Thanks so much for sharing your holidays with
me! I love the Christmas season most of all
and knowing that I am spending it with
you makes it even more special.

I hope you have the merriest of Christmases,
and remember, this year . . .

Be Blessed not Stressed.

*Jeanne M Bice*

Believe · Celebrate · Dream

To all of my Quackers,
friends and family,
who have been the wind
beneath my duck wings.

Welcome to Jeanne Bice's Quacker Factory
Christmas. For more information about Jeanne
Bice or the Quacker Factory, log on to:

www.quackerfactory.com

# Jeanne Bice's
# Quacker Factory
# Christmas

## Simple Recipes, Fabulous Parties and Decorations to Put Sparkle, Not Stress, into Your Season

Jeanne Bice
Founder of the Quacker Factory

Health Communications, Inc.
Deerfield Beach, Florida

www.hcibooks.com

**Library of Congress Cataloging-in-Publication Data
is available from the Library of Congress.**

©2006 Jeanne Bice
ISBN 0-7573-0574-1

Publisher: Health Communications, Inc.
          3201 S.W. 15th Street
          Deerfield Beach, FL 33442–8190

*Cover Photo—Paul Greco*
*Original Quacker Factory Artwork by Jodi Del-Rossi Pedri*
*Cover and inside designs by Larissa Hise Henoch*
*Inside book formatting by Lawna Patterson Oldfield*
*Inside Photos ©HCI, Getty Images, Photo Disc, Index Open, Jupiterimages*

# Contents

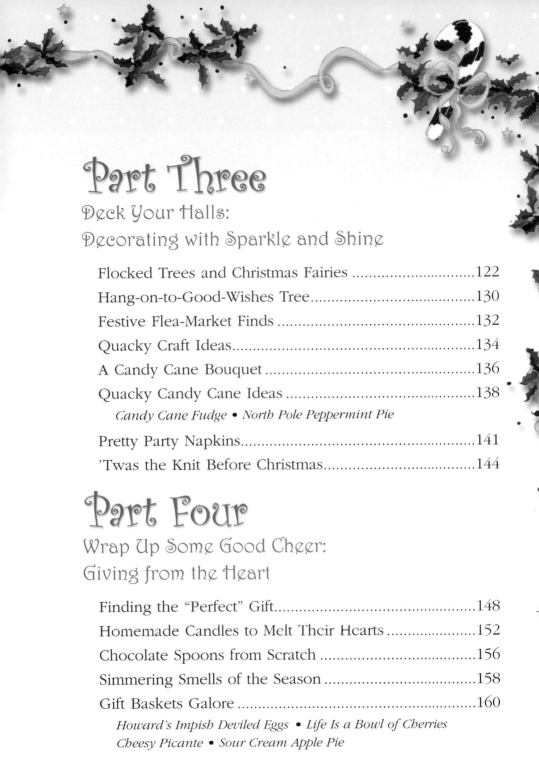

# Part Three
## Deck Your Halls:
## Decorating with Sparkle and Shine

# Part Four
## Wrap Up Some Good Cheer:
## Giving from the Heart

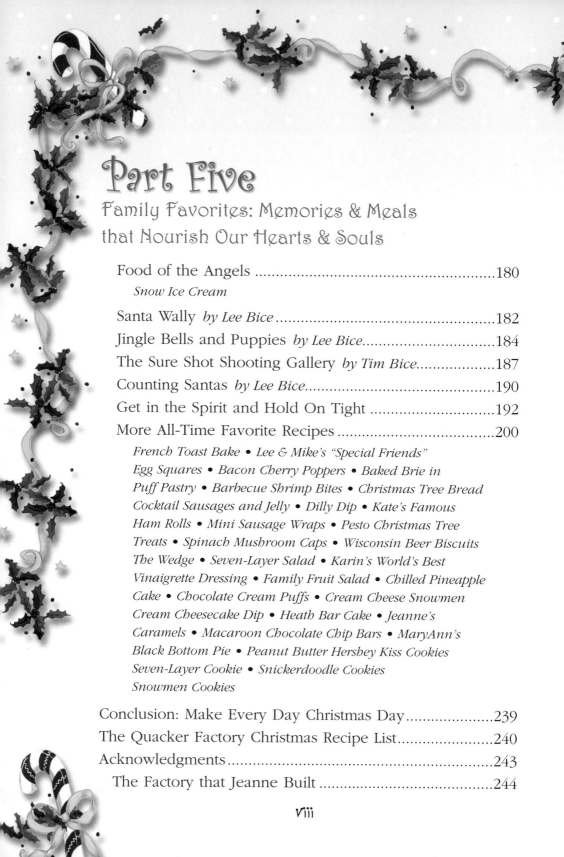

# Part Five

## Family Favorites: Memories & Meals that Nourish Our Hearts & Souls

# Introduction

**I**n order to understand my love for Christmas, you need to realize that I was created by a "Bah humbugger."

My mom was born in Scotland and had her best years as a child. When her dad died very suddenly when she was eight, her whole life changed in an instant. Her mother was given $5,000 by her late husband's family and told to leave or they would take her children away. So she and her two small children moved to Canada where she met a man the first week she arrived and married him out of fear of being alone. The family moved to North Dakota and used her $5,000 to buy a farm. Needless to say, they were very poor and Christmas was never in their budget.

Because of her upbringing, my mom has only one Christmas memory. One summer her stepfather's sister came to the farm for a visit and gave my mom a rag doll as a gift. Oh, my mom loved this doll, and it was never out of her grasp or sight . . . for the week. But when the woman left, the doll disappeared, too. My mom looked and looked, and cried and cried, but she couldn't find it any- where. She had almost forgotten about the doll a few months later. Sure enough, on Christmas morning, she opened a plain-looking box with her name on it and, like magic, the doll reappeared as her gift from Santa. Usually, all she got was an apple and an orange. It was a very bittersweet holiday that year!

Now, my dad, on the other hand, was just as poor as Mom was growing up. He also lived on a farm, in mid-Wisconsin with no electricity, no indoor toilets and no modern conveniences. Even so, his home was filled with the Christmas spirit. Grandpa would go out to the woods and cut down a tree, pulling it back to the house with his horses. He'd bring it in through the front door and set it up in the parlor, a room they only used on special occasions.

The whole family worked together decorating the tree with popcorn and berry garlands and old glass ornaments brought over from Germany many years before by great-grandparents. Then, on Christmas Eve they'd clip candles on the tree as lights, and the whole family would gather in the parlor. It was so special. . . . The candles only flickered for a very short time, but it was well worth it. Then they'd all sing "Silent Night" and blow out the candles. The room would be filled with a soft glow from the kerosene lanterns, the spirit of Christmas and the love of a family.

When I was a child, we always went to my dad's parents' home for the holidays. There was lots of laughter, lots of love, lots of food and lots of noise. You put that many Freunds together and it's loud! Think fifty people with loud mouths like mine—and many of them were auctioneers.

As you can see, my parents learned love in very different ways. Even though my mom never really liked Christmas, her "bah humbug" attitude became a running family joke, and we made it a joyful part of our holiday. She always had her "Bah Humbug" aprons and towels hanging in the kitchen. She even had a toilet seat cover that "bah humbugged."

And, God love this woman . . . our home became the place to come for Christmas dinner after my grandparents could no longer do it. She fed the whole world on Christmas day with great love and care. She took her pits and made fruit salad out of them. I'm sure she would've had you over to our house at Christmas. (I love you, Mom. . . . You gave us grit and many happy Christmases. You taught us a dollop of whipping cream makes everything in life so much sweeter!)

Since I grew up loving Christmas, and I make my business helping women decorate themselves, I decided to share what I've learned in a book about holiday entertaining the Quacker way: with lots of fun but little fuss. I'm here to tell you that Christmas is the season to sparkle, not to stress. I will show you how to make that happen.

Here I've collected my most-requested how-tos for creating a memorable holiday of your own: scrumptiously simple recipes, fabulously fun parties and decorations that anyone can make. These ideas and inspirations will help you "quack up" your holidays, from meeting new neighbors by hosting a (calorie-free) cookie exchange party or giving your budget a break with a home-made gift of simmering potpourri to making a perfect no-lumps, never-fail gravy without breaking a sweat.

So set your busy and hectic life aside for a few hours and let's celebrate Christmas!

*Quack a Smile*

*May the joy and beauty of the holiday season remain with you and yours the whole year through!*

# Part One

Seize the Spirit of the Season:
Finding the Magic in the Madness

# Don't Let the Turkeys Get You Down

o matter how hard you try and no matter how much stress you put on yourself and your dear family, Christmas is not always going to turn out perfectly. You can do every single thing I suggest in this book, plus a few old wives' tales, plus all of your girlfriends' suggestions, and it can still all "go to hell in a hand basket," as my grandpa used to say. Want proof?

One Christmas we were having our typical houseful of people over: The entire Bice family; our in-laws, the Grahams; our dear friend Lori and her daughter; plus anyone else we could think of.

That year, my son Tim and I had shows on QVC during Thanksgiving, so we didn't have the chance to host a traditional turkey dinner at the house like we usually did. So instead we decided we'd make all the Thanksgiving fixin's for Christmas, which called for only the best spread we could produce. We planned and planned and planned.

During the season I'd been watching QVC, as usual, and saw a large deep fryer. Well, you know I just *had* to have it. I'd heard that deep-frying a turkey was the best, and I was determined to give it a try. I ordered the fryer and within a few days it was at the doorstep. I called Lori and told her we needed to take it for a test-fry! We decided that she would be the turkey chef extraordinaire, the one in charge of figuring it all out.

The next day Lori arrived at the house with all the supplies and set about the big "turkey test." The turkey came out crisp and brown on the outside and tender and juicy on the inside. I have to tell you . . . it was close to the best thing I've ever tasted. It always seemed to me that the turkey breast got a little dry by the time the dark meat was done when cooked in the oven, but not in the deep fryer. And, surprisingly, it wasn't the least bit greasy. Well, Lori's turkey was a huge success so we added it to our Thanksgiving-for-Christmas menu right on the spot.

Christmas Day dawned a bit gloomy, but we weren't worried about the deep-fried turkey. What could possibly go wrong?

Lori and I had been cooking for days, and we had enough food to feed a small town. We were going to roast a turkey, make a big pot of homemade mashed potatoes and gravy, a big batch of sausage stuffing, sweet potatoes, roast prime rib, green bean casserole, cranberry sauce, rolls and, of course, my famous coleslaw. The pièce de résistance was going to be the deep-fried turkey with a huge helping of prayer that the bad weather held off.

Preparation was well under way, and it was only an hour and a half until dinner. Deep-frying a turkey takes about an hour, so it was time to get the oil heating. So far, so good . . . the weather was holding off and we knew we were going to make it! An hour before dinner, the turkey was in the oil, bubbling away like crazy. Wouldn't you know it, fifteen minutes later the sky opened up and rain came pelting down. As you know, water and hot oil don't mix, and after a few minutes of grease splattering everywhere and the gas fire going out, sweet Lori was mumbling something under her breath that would probably have made a sailor blush! We were in a pickle. *What to do?*

We moved the whole operation into the garage. Now, I know this is frowned upon . . . fire hazard and all . . . but what choice did we have? We had to save that turkey! After we moved everything, we lit the gas back up and got it going again. Unfortunately, the oil had cooled a lot, so it took a while to get it back up to temperature. Meanwhile, the turkey was taking a grease-bath the entire time and, unbeknownst to us, the bird had continued to cook even though the oil had cooled.

Once the oil was going again, we refigured the cooking time and decided it had another forty-five minutes, since that was how much time was left when the fire went out. Even though the entire dinner was being delayed to wait for the fried turkey, that was okay. . . . It would be well worth it when our guests tasted this holiday masterpiece.

Forty-five minutes later, Lori removed the turkey from the fryer and brought it in. Oh, it was beautiful . . . deep golden brown and crispy. The rest of our dinner had been laid out, and it was time to cut into this beautiful bird. With everyone standing around, Lori made a big production of sharpening the knife and preparing to cut. Well, you could have knocked us over with a turkey feather at this point! Instead of the light stream of juices we had expected, the first cut into the breast of the turkey produced a kind of "poof." A small cloud of what can only be described as turkey dust shot out of the cut, and the smell wafting out of the bird was less than wondrous.

Lori peeked inside the turkey skin, and all she saw were the charred remains of a once-proud turkey. She had made a *slight* miscalculation with the time and cooked it too long. At this point, the excitement had been building among the guests, and they were clamoring to see this amazing creation that Lori and I had endlessly bragged about. Needless to say, the laughter and ribbing Lori took for the rest of the day about the "Great Turkey Test" only added to the festiveness of the occasion.

Everyone was wonderful; we tossed the turkey in the garbage and dove into all the other food. We didn't get our fried turkey that year, but we did get a valuable lesson: It doesn't matter what the weather is like, or what's on your table—it's *who* you spend the holidays with that really matters! So let it all go. Enjoy your holidays no matter what happens. And remember, even chaotic times can create good memories. It's up to you to see your experiences as bad . . . or blessed. Enjoy.

Quack a Smile

These are the days
we will remember forever.

# Deep-Fried

## TURKEY MENU

Deep-Fried Turkey

Corn Cheese Bake

Stuffing Made Simple

"Eat Your Green Beans" Casserole

Sweet Potato Casserole

Hearty Mashed Potatoes

Mom's Christmas Salad

Jeanne's Amazing Gravy

Pumpkin Cookies

# Deep-Fried Turkey

To figure out how much oil to use, put the turkey in the fryer basket and place in the pot. Add water until it reaches 1 to 2 inches above the turkey; take out the turkey and note the water line. Pour out the water and dry the pot thoroughly. Add smoke-free oil to your mark (usually around 5 quarts).

Start the oil heating at least half an hour to 45 minutes before cooking (the oil should reach about 350 to 365 degrees). You can inject marinades into your turkey, but never stuff a turkey that is being fried. Dry the turkey off completely before submerging in the oil. Put the turkey in the fryer basket and SLOWLY lower into the oil. Whole turkeys need about 3 minutes per pound to cook. Then add 5 minutes to the total time. The internal temperature should be 180 degrees in the thigh area and 170 degrees in the breast area. I use a meat thermometer with a very long handle!

When it's done, remove from oil and let it drip for a few minutes to get out the excess oil. Take the turkey out of the basket and place it on a platter. Let it cool for a few minutes and then cut 'er up.

quacky Tip

It's best to do a couple of test runs before you debut your fried turkey for a crowd of hungry guests. Use a turkey under 14 pounds for best results. And, as we learned, you might want to have a back-up plan!

# Never Too Much

I tend to cook much more food than I need because you have to have enough left over to make a turkey, dressing, mashed potato and cranberry sauce sandwich the next day. And why not throw a little gravy on top? It's only Christmas once a year!

And, truth be told, I always cook too much for the number of people coming over no matter what the season. Probably because of my Aunt Lena and then my own mother.

As a child, I remember going over to my Aunt Lena and Uncle Joe's house. Aunt Lena was the best cook, but when she got very old she began to really underestimate how much food she needed. We'd leave, and my mother would grumble, "How did she expect ten people to get enough to eat when she only cooked a two-pound chicken?" We'd all laugh and go home and have a sandwich.

Years later when my mom and dad got much older, six of us went to their home for dinner. My dad said the prayer and with great gusto thanked my mom for the "big feast" she had set before us. He said there was so much food we'd be eating leftovers for days. Well, she had made three pork chops, two baked sweet potatoes and a small bowl of homemade applesauce—for eight people! My husband Butchie's family used to say "FHB," which meant Family Hold Back. So we said "FHB," and yes, *they* would have left-overs for lunch the next day. The rest of us would stop at a fast-food restaurant on the way home.

But, I digress. . . . Believe me, I have not hit that stage in my cooking yet. I still make enough food to feed the entire states of Wisconsin, Pennsylvania and Florida.

# Corn Cheese Bake

### Makes 6 side-dish servings

This was my brother Dick's favorite recipe growing up. He loved, loved, loved cream corn, and this was his favorite variation on it.

1 3-oz. package cream cheese, softened
¼ cup milk
1 tablespoon butter or margarine
½ teaspoon onion salt
One 1-pound can of whole kernel corn, drained
Paprika

Preheat oven to 350 degrees. Combine cream cheese, milk, butter and onion salt in a saucepan; stir over low heat until cheese melts. Stir corn into cheese. Pour into small casserole dish. Sprinkle with paprika. Cook uncovered until bubbly, about 10 minutes.

# Gotta Have Stuffing

My mom was born in Scotland, and as a Scottish lass, she never learned to cook. So when she married my German father, she had to learn to cook. Luckily her new mother-in-law, Grandma Freund, was the nicest, sweetest, kindest woman. She taught my mom to be a great German cook. I think her turkey dressing is the best in the whole world.

About a week before Thanksgiving, my mom would set a cookie sheet on top of the refrigerator and lay leftover bread and rolls on it. She liked to dry the bread out in chunks, but not too small. She always felt that store-bought stuffing was too small. Now, this is the step that always made me chuckle. After drying out the bread, go figure, the day of the "dressing making" she would get up in the morning and put the bread in a big blue roasting pan . . . the kind that all of our moms had. You know, the long, rectangular one with the big lid.

Then, she would add milk and chicken stock 'til it was sort of soft. She used to make her own chicken stock from the neck and gizzard. (Now, thank God, you can buy it in a box or a can at the grocery store!) She'd get in there with both hands and squish it up. Remember, when cooking, God gave you the perfect tools: your own two hands. Just get in there and smash away. . . . It relieves stress! It's like playing in the dirt as a child. After properly smashing away, my mom would let the mixture sit for a while to absorb.

She would then take a real large onion and chop it up—not too small. Then she'd put some butter in a real large frying pan. My grandma had an old cast-iron pan that Mom would use, but I go for something a bit lighter. She would then cook the onions until they were translucent. While they were bubbling away, she would add some sausage. (I like the mild kind, but if you're a zingy family, you can use the hot. "Germans aren't big on hot!")

When the sausage was all brown and pretty, it was time to mix it into the bread. Now this is where the German heritage comes out in this recipe: Throw in some butter—about half a stick. Just cut it up and mix it in.

We'd never stuff the turkey with the dressing. Mom always left the stuffing in her big blue roaster. She'd just wipe down the sides as it was cooking so the pan didn't burn. Then she would sprinkle a package of dry pork gravy mix on the top, which made it very rich. She would put it in the oven by 8:30 A.M. to bake at 350 degrees. She baked and stirred, baked and stirred so that the top got crunchy and crispy. She just kept turning the crispy top into the dressing. It would get dryer as it cooked, so she would keep adding

*quacky* Tip

Whether you like your stuffing spicy or mild, this recipe is the best! You can make it a day ahead and just re-warm it. I think it's even better the second day. I'll sometimes add chopped water chestnuts for more crunch.

chicken stock. Over the years as I have made this, I have found that adding a jar of turkey gravy as I go along really makes it yummy.

At around 2:00 P.M., she would put my dad to tasting to make sure it had hit perfection. After he gave it the go-ahead, she would move the dressing into a pretty casserole or two, and set it on top of the stove until dinnertime. Right before serving, she'd pop it back into the oven to make sure it was piping hot. If it got too dry, she'd add a bit more stock or gravy.

When I roast a turkey in the oven, I stuff it with a big onion and a big apple. I don't peel either one. I salt and pepper the outside of the bird, and away it goes. If you aren't feeling particularly creative or if you need more on quantities, *Better Homes and Gardens* has a great recipe in their cookbook!

Make each recipe your own so that it makes your taste buds dance! Life is all about being creative. A dab of this, a smidge of that, a dollop of love and a pinch of joy.

# Stuffing Made Simple

1 stick of butter
1 large onion, chopped
1 or 2 tubes of Jimmy Dean sausage
½ pound Italian sausage (optional)
1 package herbed bread cubes
   (or 1 pound stale bread)
1 cup chicken stock
1 cup milk
½ teaspoon salt
½ teaspoon black pepper
1 package of dry pork gravy mix

In a skillet over medium heat, melt half a stick of butter. Slowly fry the onions until they are translucent. Add the Jimmy Dean sausage and the Italian sausage if you are using it and fry until nicely browned. Break the sausage up with a fork and remove from heat.

Pour the bread cubes into a large roasting pan. Add the chicken stock and milk, and mix with your hands until it's moist. Add the sausage and onions. Add the other ½ stick of butter, cut up in slices. Your mixture should be moist, but not wet. If not moist enough, add a bit more chicken stock and let it sit until it's absorbed. Pour the packet of dry gravy mix on the top and bake at 350 degrees for at least 5 hours, baking and stirring. If it gets too dry, add a bit more stock.

I'll use this recipe for a turkey or a crown roast of pork. When I do a crown roast, I throw some in the center because I really love how it looks!

# "Eat Your Green Beans" Casserole

### Makes about 12 servings

My son, Tim, loves the old standby green bean casserole, but it's just not one of my favorites.
So, I always have to do the "bean thing" for him, corn casserole for me and fresh asparagus for my daughter-in-law, Karin. That's way too many veggies for one gathering.

6 tablespoons butter, divided
3 tablespoons all-purpose flour
1 teaspoon salt
1 teaspoon sugar
¼ cup onion, chopped fine
1 cup heavy cream
1 pound sliced fresh mushrooms
1 pound fresh green beans, cleaned and ends trimmed
2 cups shredded cheddar cheese
1 large can french fried onions

Preheat oven to 350 degrees. Melt 3 tablespoons butter in a large skillet over medium heat. Stir in flour until smooth and cook for about a minute. Stir in salt, sugar, onion and heavy cream, and the mixture will start to thicken.

In a separate skillet, melt 3 tablespoons butter and add the mushrooms and green beans. Cover and simmer slowly for

about 6 minutes or until beans
are starting to soften.

Pour the mixture in first
skillet into a 2½-quart casserole
dish. Add the mushrooms and
green beans and stir gently to
coat. Spread shredded cheese
over the top and bake for
20 minutes.

Open the oven and
spread the french
fried onions over
the top; bake for
an additional
10 minutes.

quacky

Tip

If you're really lazy,
Stouffer's now has it all made
for you! Just scoop it out into
one of your favorite casserole
dishes and it looks like you slaved
over a hot stove all day. A string
bean hanging off the end of your
nose really adds to the realism!

# Sweet Potato Casserole

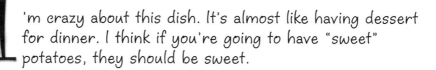

## Makes about 8 servings

I'm crazy about this dish. It's almost like having dessert for dinner. I think if you're going to have "sweet" potatoes, they should be sweet.

6 large sweet potatoes, baked,
   peeled and mashed
3 eggs
1 1/4 cups milk
1/4 cup bourbon
3/4 cup white sugar
3/4 cup brown sugar
1/2 teaspoon salt
1 teaspoon cinnamon
1/2 teaspoon allspice
2 teaspoons vanilla
1/2 cup crushed pecans (optional)
Mini marshmallows

Preheat oven to 350 degrees. Mix all ingredients except marshmallows and beat well, until light and fluffy. If needed, add a little more milk. Spoon sweet potato mixture into a buttered casserole dish; bake for 20 to 30 minutes until the potatoes are set. Add the mini marshmallows to the top and bake another few minutes until marshmallows are melted and lightly browned. This makes about 8 big servings, but is easily doubled and tripled!

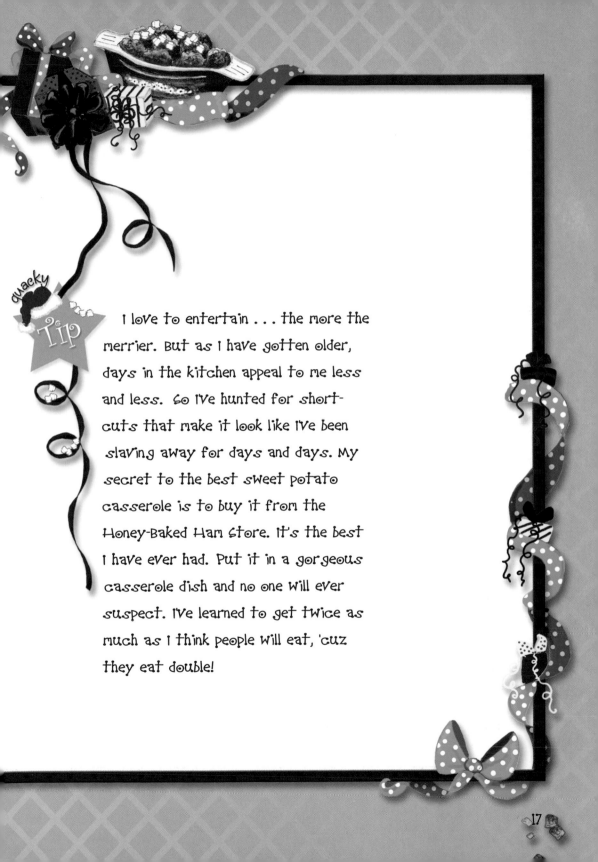

quacky Tip

I love to entertain . . . the more the merrier. But as I have gotten older, days in the kitchen appeal to me less and less. So I've hunted for short-cuts that make it look like I've been slaving away for days and days. My secret to the best sweet potato casserole is to buy it from the Honey-Baked Ham Store. It's the best I have ever had. Put it in a gorgeous casserole dish and no one will ever suspect. I've learned to get twice as much as I think people will eat, 'cuz they eat double!

## Spectacular Spuds Without the Stress

Mashed potatoes are the one thing that always have to be done at the last minute at a holiday meal. Sure, you can make a mashed potato casserole the day before and bake it in the oven, but it's not the same as creamy mashed potatoes. They are the best part of the meal. Here's a tip I learned many years ago that has helped to take the stress out of last-minute preparation of the holiday meal.

I peel my potatoes the day before and cover them with very cold water (I add ice to the water and put them in the refrigerator overnight). When I go to cook the potatoes, I dump out the water and rinse them well; then add fresh water for cooking. Be sure to add a little salt to the water because if you don't cook the potatoes in salt water, you can never get them seasoned well.

A few hours before the big rush comes, I cook the potatoes until they are tender, while warming my milk and getting out some butter. Drain the potatoes when they're cooked, making sure they are all done: Usually there are a few uncooked ones in the batch, and one bad potato can spoil the whole pot!

After I drain them, I put them back on the burner to "bloom" them. Just shake the pan back and forth 'til all the extra water is gone. This ensures the potatoes are dry.

*My mother was a real stickler about the food being "hot." Many a meal got sent back in a restaurant because she felt it was cold. So the "gotta-be-hot" thing is in my head. And, you know what? YOU are hot!*

Once the water is gone, I mash the potatoes with my portable electric beater or mixer, adding milk and butter very slowly. Remember, you can always add more, but you can't take away. If you add too much, they get soupy . . . but you also don't want them to get sticky either. Take your time 'til you've reached perfection.

Now, taste! This is an important step. Do they need a little more salt? Now is the time to do it. Remember, though, that your gravy has salt in it too. Now here comes the trick for super-moist potatoes: Set the pot back on the stove but don't turn the burner on. Then put a dish towel over the top of the pot and then put the lid back on. This keeps the moisture out of the potatoes.

Job well-done. You can now move on, knowing your potatoes will be perfect when you are ready to serve them.

# Hearty Mashed Potatoes

10 pounds baking potatoes, peeled and
    cut into small chunks
2/3 cup butter
1 cup milk or more to your liking
    (pick your favorite: fat free for lighter or
    whole milk or half & half for creamier)
Salt and pepper to taste

In a very large stock pot bring salted water to a boil. Add the potatoes and cook for 15 to 20 minutes until they are soft, but not too mushy. Remove from heat and drain the water. Put pot back on the burner for a few minutes, shaking it to eliminate the excess water. Add the rest of the ingredients slowly and mash with a potato masher or beat with an electric mixer. Salt and pepper to taste.

quacky Tip

You can also add sour cream, cheese, chives or even bacon to this recipe . . . that's the beauty of it. Make it your own and create your own family favorite.

20

# Mom's Christmas Salad

Some of the most wonderful recipes in my collection came from my mother. She would try things out and really work on them until they were absolutely perfect.

- ¼ cup red cinnamon candy
- 1 package (3 oz.) cherry Jell-O
- 1 cup hot water
- 1 ½ cups sweet applesauce
- 1 package (8 oz.) cream cheese
- ½ cup nuts (your choice)
- ½ cup celery
- ½ cup mayonnaise

Melt candy in hot water. Add Jell-O and applesauce. Put half of mixture in a Jell-O mold. In a separate bowl, mix cream cheese, nuts, celery and mayonnaise. When the first layer of Jell-O is set, put the nut and cream cheese mixture in the mold as the next layer. Then add the remaining Jell-O layer. This comes out red and white like Santa himself.

# Jeanne's Amazing Gravy

**I**f there is anything I've ever learned it's that you have to make a ton of gravy, and since a turkey will only give you so much juice, it's not cheating to buy store-bought and doctor it up. It makes everything on the table taste a little better. And, you have to be sure that you make enough to cover all the leftovers!

2 cups Swanson Chicken Broth
6 jars of premade turkey gravy
4 packets of dry turkey gravy mix
All the drippings from the roasting turkey
Sherry or cognac as needed
   (some for the cook, too!)
Salt and pepper to taste

In a large saucepan, heat the chicken broth and turkey gravy, stirring as it simmers. Add the drippings from the turkey and stir some more. Add ¼ cup of cognac and reserve the rest. Turn up the heat until your mixture is just at the boiling point. Turn it down to simmer, and s-l-o-w-l-y add the packets of dry gravy, stirring constantly. Continue to stir to avoid lumps. Adjust at this point if it is too thick or too thin. (I like it a little thicker.) Add the rest of the cognac or sherry for flavor to your liking.

I like to put gravy out on the table in ironstone pitchers instead of gravy boats. The gravy boats are so small that you are forever getting up from the table to refill them. The pitchers are beautiful and sturdy and are easily passed from guest to guest around your table. Wait until the last minute, after the prayer, to bring the gravy to the table. That way, if anything has cooled off a bit, the gravy will warm it back up.

# Pumpkin Cookies

### Makes about 8 dozen

2 cups sugar
2 cups butter
2 eggs
2 teaspoons vanilla extract
15-oz. can pumpkin
4 cups all-purpose flour

2 teaspoons baking powder
2 teaspoons baking soda
1 teaspoon salt
1 teaspoon cinnamon
1 teaspoon nutmeg

Preheat oven to 350 degrees. Cream first 4 ingredients together; stir in pumpkin. Mix well; set aside. Sift remaining ingredients together, and then gradually mix into pumpkin mixture until well blended. Drop by teaspoonfuls onto greased baking sheets; bake 10 to 15 minutes. Cool and then frost.

Quick Caramel Frosting:
  ½ cup butter
  ½ cup brown sugar, packed
  ¼ cup milk
  1 teaspoon vanilla extract
  1 ¾ cups powdered sugar

Heat butter and brown sugar until melted and dissolved; remove from heat. Pour into a mixing bowl; blend in milk and vanilla. Stir in enough powdered sugar for desired spreading consistency.

# Freund Family Christmas Breakfast

While everyone loves Christmas dinner, if you think about it, Christmas breakfast can be the best meal of the season. It's just your family and the anticipation of what's waiting for you under the tree. All of the work is done—even Santa is finished with all of his jobs. As the house comes alive on Christmas morning, spirits are high. Everyone is together, ready to see what's under the tree. My dad's favorite meal was always breakfast, so on Christmas Day he made it really special.

When I was a little girl, I truly believed I could hear the reindeer on the roof on Christmas Eve. More likely it was just my dad rummaging through the attic getting out the tree stuff! Santa always came to our house on Christmas Eve when he'd put up the tree and then leave presents. So instead of "On Dasher, On Dancer, On Prancer," we'd hear my dad moaning and groaning!

On Christmas morning, we absolutely could *not* go downstairs until my folks came and got us. Then, we'd all go down into the living room together and turn on the tree. First it was the excitement of seeing the tree for the first time. Since gifts from Santa were never wrapped, we'd *ooh* and *ahh* over what Santa left for us . . . but no touching! We could only look as we walked past the tree into the dining room for breakfast.

My mom always had pumpkin kuchen and brats on the table. Every day of our life we drank orange juice with castor oil, which I hated. On Christmas morning, we got to skip the castor oil and OJ, and instead Mom gave us mugs of white hot chocolate with big puffy marshmallows. Dad would light a fire in the fireplace, and the tree and presents were in full view.

Instead of counting carbs and calories
this season, count your blessings.

We ate and talked about what made Christmas so special for each of us. This time together was almost better than the presents (almost). After the holiday pace had softened, this was the time we could unwind and enjoy the *real* magic of Christmas. Nothing beats Christmas morning breakfast. . . . It's magical.

# The Freund Family

## BREAKFAST MENU

Freund Pumpkin Kuchen

Breakfast Brats

White Christmas Hot Chocolate

Santa-Needs-Some-Caffeine
Christmas Coffee

# Freund Pumpkin Kuchen

**T**his is one of those recipes you won't find in a book (except this one). My mom learned it from my dad's mom, and it had been passed down by generations before her. There are no real measurements and no wrong way to do it. Best of all, you have to practice to do it well, and it always tastes great, even if it doesn't look so good.

One loaf frozen sweet bread dough
16-oz. can pumpkin pie filling
Butter (you can never have enough)

Preheat your oven to 350 degrees and butter a 9-inch round cake tin.

Thaw sweet bread dough and let it rise per package instructions. Tear off a small piece of dough and press it flat onto the cake tin until it's very thin (almost see-through). Continue breaking off and pressing small pieces into the tin until you cover the entire bottom; as you go halfway up the sides of the tin, make the dough a bit thicker.

Take the pumpkin pie filling and mix it up according to the instructions on the can. Spread a layer about ½-inch thick onto the sweet bread dough.

Place in the oven and cook about 20 minutes until the pie filling is set and the crust is golden brown (the edges will puff). Let cool and dig in.

Being from Wisconsin, the dairy state, we eat everything with butter. So be sure and have plenty of fresh creamery butter on hand and watch these traditional German goodies disappear!

Oh, my mouth is watering just writing this! This might be an acquired family taste. My daughter and son crave it, but at my age, it gives me heartburn. But it's so worth it.

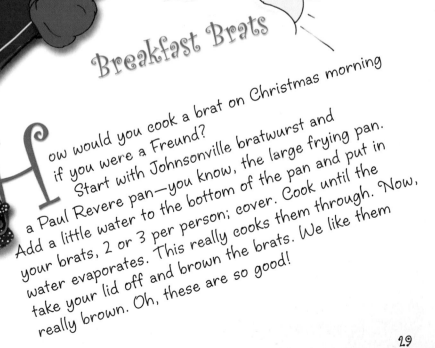

## Breakfast Brats

How would you cook a brat on Christmas morning if you were a Freund? Start with Johnsonville bratwurst and a Paul Revere pan—you know, the large frying pan. Add a little water to the bottom of the pan and put in your brats, 2 or 3 per person; cover. Cook until the water evaporates. This really cooks them through. Now, take your lid off and brown the brats. We like them really brown. Oh, these are so good!

# White Christmas Hot Chocolate

### Makes about 4 cups

This is a very "Christmassy" recipe for hot chocolate. The rest of the year we make our hot chocolate a bit differently, but at Christmas we go all out! Even some of the adults will pass on coffee and go for the hot chocolate!

   12 oz. of milk (I make it really creamy
       with whole milk)
   1 ¼ oz. of finely chopped white chocolate
   1 oz. of crushed peppermint or
       spearmint candy canes

Pour milk into a saucepan and bring it to a simmer over medium heat. Reduce heat to medium-low. Add the chocolate, half of the crushed candy canes and a pinch of salt. Whisk until smooth and creamy, and then pour into a coffee mug. Sprinkle the rest of the crushed candy cane on top.

## quacky Tip

Make your juice glasses sparkle on Christmas Day: Dip the rims in water and roll in coarse sugar before filling with orange juice.

# Santa-Needs-Some-Caffeine Christmas Coffee

### Makes about 10 cups

I make this mixture ahead of time and just add it to my coffee pot after I have brewed my coffee. It's great for mornings or for after-Christmas dinner. Your family and guests will love it.

½ cup sugar
⅓ cup water
¼ cup unsweetened cocoa
¼ teaspoon cinnamon
1 pinch grated nutmeg
1 pot of coffee (10 cups)

In a small saucepan, heat water until it is at a low boil. Add sugar, cocoa, cinnamon and nutmeg. Boil for 2 minutes at a low boil and reduce heat. Simmer for 10 minutes.

Right before you are ready to serve, make your pot of coffee. Add your holiday mixture to your favorite coffee and serve.

# Cut Out the Cut-Out Cookies

**M**aking cut-out cookies is always something a mother thinks she should do with her children during the holidays. Well, let me tell you, it's one of those "shoulds" that could kill you. You are just too busy!

For years, thank you, God, Grandma Bice had all the kids at her house for a day of cookie baking. She took the "should" off my shoulders. Then one year she said she was just too old to continue the tradition—but my kids still thought they should get to do this. I decided we had to come up with a solution.

Why not bake cookies for Valentine's Day, Easter and Christmas in July? All of these holidays call for special-shaped cookies, and there's typically not as much stress at these times of the year.

Believe me, when the kids are out of school for the summer and you start hearing "I'm bored!"

quacky Tip

Encourage your kids to invite friends over to make the cookies with you. Remember, if friends come, make sure the moms stay so they get to share the experience with their kids. Plus, you <u>do</u> need a little help and some girl-friendly conversation.

this is a great thing to do. My kids loved making Christmas cookies in July: They either sold them from their lemonade stand or we'd plan a Christmas in July party.

All of our friends enjoyed the cookies more in the summer. There wasn't so much other stuff around to eat like there is at Christmas . . . lots less guilt! And, for some reason, guiltless cookies sure taste a lot better.

So, if your "shoulds" are getting you down, come up with a new way you "could" do it. Be a dreamer!

# On-a-Roll
# Roll-Out Cookies
### Makes 12 dozen

1 tablespoon plus 1 teaspoon baking soda

2 cups sour cream

4 cups butter, softened

4 cups sugar

8 eggs, beaten

2 teaspoons vanilla extract

4 teaspoons baking powder

12 cups all-purpose flour

Preheat oven to 325 degrees. Mix baking soda into sour cream. Add butter and sugar. Mix well. Stir in eggs and vanilla; then mix in baking powder and flour. Chill for at least one hour.

Roll dough out to ¼-inch thickness. Cut with cookie cutters and place on greased, floured baking sheets.

Bake for 8-10 minutes. Let cool. Spread frosting over the tops.

Frosting:

Two 1-pound packages powdered sugar

2 cups butter, softened

2 to 4 teaspoons vanilla extract

8-oz. package cream cheese, softened

¼ to ½ cup milk

Mix sugar, butter, vanilla and cream cheese together. Add enough milk to make the desired thickness.

## Money Isn't Everything

This season, do yourself a favor and remember that the holiday are not about the getting or the giving. One year in the late nineties my family learned this lesson firsthand. Back then, we were going through a bad time in our business. Just worrying about putting food on the table was a big job. There was nothing left over to buy Christmas gifts . . . not even a bag of candy. *What was I going to do? How were we going to get through the season?*

Well, we sat down and had a family confab. How could we make Christmas special with no money? We put on our creative hats and talked about what we could make. While we had the inspiration to have a crafty Christmas, there was a big hurdle: I didn't have any money for craft supplies.

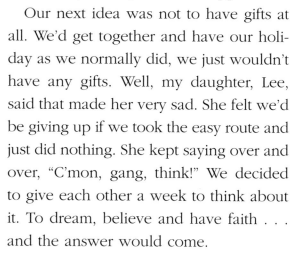

Our next idea was not to have gifts at all. We'd get together and have our holiday as we normally did, we just wouldn't have any gifts. Well, my daughter, Lee, said that made her very sad. She felt we'd be giving up if we took the easy route and just did nothing. She kept saying over and over, "C'mon, gang, think!" We decided to give each other a week to think about it. To dream, believe and have faith . . . and the answer would come.

I went home, and as I walked around my house, I thought, *Why not share what I have?* My daughter had often admired my cut-glass, saying, "Hey, Mom, please leave your cut-glass stuff to me." So I picked out four special pieces that had great stories to go with them. One was a tall cut-glass vase that my late husband's aunt gave us just before she died. She had received it as a wedding present in 1901 from a couple who lived on the farm next to hers. They had received the vase as a wedding gift fifty years before they gave it to my husband's aunt. The family that gave it to them brought it over from the old country. I wrote a story about each piece, wrapped them up really pretty and gave them from my heart with lots of love.

Whenever we were in the kitchen, my son Tim would say, "What I need is some cast-iron frying pans like you have. The food always tastes so much better in them." I'd always tell him to go buy some. He'd say he didn't want to do that because it wouldn't be the same. Mine had been seasoned for years by Grandma and Grandpa and my mom. They had years and years of good food built in them.

## Quack a Smile

Santa, save a little time . . .

put me under naughty.

So I picked out four of my favorite cast-iron pieces from my mom and my dad's mom. I wrote up recipes that worked well with them: My brother's fried fish from the fishing camps of Canada, my mom's fried chicken and a friend's hot, hot bacon-cheese corn bread. I wrote these on really nice recipe cards that I made myself, wrapped them up really pretty and gave them from my heart with lots of love.

Because my daughter-in-law, Karin, is a great cook, I gave her my antique pot-de-crème cups, a set of twelve. I also gave her the recipe for pot-de-crème to use at her parties, even though at the time it didn't seem like we'd ever have parties again on our budget. And I gave her an antique tea set from Grandma Bice. I wrapped them up really pretty and gave them from my heart with lots of love.

I did this for everyone on my list. They received each gift with love in their hearts for me and gave back lots of love.

But I think the best gift any of us came up with was Tim and Karin's gift to my daughter, Lee. Lee doesn't have a green thumb, but she loves to look at beautiful flowers. Karin, on the other hand, is a great gardener. One day Karin and Tim drove miles out of their way to nearby towns to find lots of plants really cheap from plant wholesalers. They took the plants to Lee's house on Christmas Day, cleaned out her flower beds, placed new dirt, fertilized and then planted all the plants. It took two full days to get the job done. It was truly a gift given with love (and sweat), and as those flowers continued to bloom all year long, Lee could feel the love whenever she looked out her window at her beautiful flowers.

So our "poorest" Christmas really turned out to be our "richest" Christmas. And the memories of that holiday spirit still live in our hearts today. I do think God let us be "poor" for awhile so that we never take anything for granted again. And we don't. It was a great lesson for our family: It's not how much you have; it's how much you love. So with love in your heart this holiday, make this season the richest one you have ever had.

*Quack a Smile*

**Let miracles find you!**

# Part Two

## Give Hassle-Free Get-Togethers: Don't Be Too Pooped to Party

# The Trim-a-Tree, Save-a-Marriage Party

Amid the hustle of the holidays, there is *that* magic moment when Christmas happens. It might be when you see the stores decorated, it might be the first time you hear "Jingle Bells" on the car radio, but for me it's when the tree is finally up in my house. I love the festive feeling the place takes on when the tree stands in my front window wishing everyone who drives by a "Happy Christmas." It's almost alive with joy.

I've always found getting and decorating the perfect tree to be the most exciting part of the holidays. The whole family would pile into the car, bundled up against the cold, singing carols all the way to the tree farm. Even my husband Butchie would chime in. We'd hit the lot with great anticipation.

In Wisconsin, farmed trees come snow-covered and frozen. When I found a likely candidate, Butch would lift it and thump it on the ground to shake off the snow and coax down its branches. After thumping ten trees, his enthusiasm would begin to wane. After fifteen trees, he'd start muttering. After twenty, his gloves would be sticky with sap, his arms would hurt, and he just wanted the whole thing over. Even the kids would whine that they

CHRISTMAS TREES 1 MiLe

were freezing and "Can't we pleeeese go home?" Not me. I hadn't found "the perfect tree." Finally, after a two-hour, subzero search with everyone, including the tree farmer, losing patience *(Where was their spirit?)* the quest would be over. I had found "the perfect tree."

I'd ask the tree man to do a fresh cut off the trunk and trim some of the bottom branches, 'cause I figured at this point that job would push Butch right over the edge.

I couldn't understand what the problem was. When I was young, they didn't have perfect trees, so after we got a lopsided one home, my dad would perform a branch transplant. He'd drill tiny holes in the trunk wherever there were gaps, then fill them with the surgically removed bottom branches. If there were any left over, we'd make a front door swag. How hard is that?

Oh, finding our tree was so much fun. The car smelled so piney. I'd want to sing "Deck the Halls!" Ooops! No singing in the car—my clan was cranky. But I was so HAPPY! I loooved Christmas!

One thing I should mention is that the tree would stand in a room with an eighteen-foot ceiling. So naturally it was huge and heavy. While I couldn't wait to get it home and make the place smell sooo good, Butch didn't share my exuberance. All he could think of was how he was going to haul the tree off the station wagon, into the house and into its stand, hoping against hope that our son, Tim, had more strength than he did the year before.

The two would wrestle the giant to the ground, then drag it to the house. Butch then faced the next big hurdle—squeezing it though the doorway. I couldn't understand why he worried so much; it managed to make it through every year. I told him to push harder! He asked for less advice from me and a little more help. Yuck! Get tree sap on my good kid-gloves—no way.

So he huffed and he puffed and he huffed some more, and of course the tree strained through. We might have had to patch and paint the door jamb a bit, but no problem . . . the tree was home! Then it had to sit for a day to thaw so I could tell if it was indeed the perfect tree.

As I scrutinized it, Butchie would pray, "Oh please, dear God, let her love this tree." He never forgot the year he had to return three trees before finding "the perfect one." He also fretted that in order to haul down the decorations, he had to clear off the attic steps because they had a year's worth of stuff on 'em, including some of the kids' presents. So he couldn't ask for their help.

Between six thousand and eight thousand tiny white lights decorated our tree every year, and all had to be untangled and tested. That job in itself took days. Then Butch had to hang all the high ornaments, making sure all the favorites were in front. All the while I'd be chirping, "This is so much fun. . . . Let's do three trees next year!"

One Christmas, after taking the usual week to set up and decorate the tree, Butch fell into bed exhausted but secure in the knowledge that I was happy and Santa had a place to deliver the presents. Late that night we awoke to a thunderous crash. The kids thought Santa had come early and tumbled down the chimney. We all ran to the atrium. There it was—our beautiful tree in a heap amid hundreds of broken ornaments. "Let's cancel Christmas," Butch pleaded. Fat chance.

We got the tree back up and redecorated, of course, and Butch learned a lesson—when setting up a towering tree, secure it to the walls and/or ceiling. Each year his mission was to figure out how.

One year it all came to a head. Keeping a work-weary tortoise (Butch) and a holiday-hyper hare (me) happy was a challenge we had to face. He just couldn't take the tree trial anymore. We fought for days. I screamed and shouted and cried and cried 'til I seemed to get my way. But he was

miserable. Where had the joy gone? Finally he announced, "Jeanne, I can't face it another year. We need to find a way to simplify this tree thing, and do it in peace. Come up with a solution."

I thought long and hard. Then it hit me: a "Trim-a-Tree party!" Many hands make light work. Besides, I could do my hostess-with-the-mostest thing, and he could put up the tree with his buddies. It could all be done in one Sunday afternoon, and it would be so much fun. Happiness was back in our soon-to-be decked halls.

Our first party was so successful it became an annual event for our family and friends. Best of all, it saved our marriage!

# The Trim-a-Tree Invitation

Over the years I've created many invitations, but this one is my favorite.

I bought a bunch of fresh Christmas wreaths from the Boy Scouts before Thanksgiving and decorated each one; then I attached an invitation to the tree trimming. Then, very early one morning, I hung each of them on my friends' front doors. The wreaths not only signaled a fun time ahead, they were rewards for the upcoming effort. Best of all, everyone loved them.

When party guests arrived on tree trimming day, we assigned groups to do various tasks. Some people tested lights, some strung lights, and we all hung ornaments while drinking a little and eating a lot. In just a few hours the job was done, and the tree stood tall and proud to greet all who saw her. Best of all, we had a ball.

Since guests work hard during the party, it's important to feed them well. Here are some of the best-loved, yet easily assembled recipes from our Trim-a-Tree party:

Please help us create holiday magic

We'll trim the tree, sing some songs, we'll eat and drink and have fun all night long.

It wouldn't be the same without you . . .

Date:      Time:

Address:

R.S.V.P.

Bring an ornament for my tree

Take one home for your tree

# Trim-A-Tree

## PARTY MENU

Eggnog

Virgin Punch

Spicy Beef Dip

Pecan Olive Dip

Bice Bacon Wraps

Chipped "Where's the Beef?" Dip

English Muffin Cheddar Bites

What-a-Ham Sandwiches

Tiny Tuna Melts

Baby BLTs

# Eggnog

### Makes approximately 20 cups

1 quart dairy eggnog
1 pint vanilla ice cream, softened
1 quart 7-Up

Just before serving, combine eggnog and softened ice cream. Slowly add 7-Up. You can add a little extra "flavor" by putting some brandy or whiskey directly into the punch. Or, if you are having guests who don't drink alcohol, you can have it handy and they can add it if they want. I always put it in a pretty decanter right next to the punch bowl.

# Virgin Punch

### Serves approximately 16 people

One 46-oz. can unsweetened pineapple juice
3 cups apricot nectar
2 cups orange juice
¼ cup lemon juice
1 quart club soda
1 quart pineapple sherbet

Chill all ingredients. Mix all four juices in a punch bowl. Just before serving, add the club soda and fold in softened sherbet.

# Spicy Beef Dip

## Makes 12 servings

This was a favorite recipe of my friend Jane Bumby Barclay. It's hearty enough to eat on hamburger buns for dinner, but I love it with crackers as an appetizer.

1 pound ground beef
½ cup chopped onions
1 clove garlic minced
One 8-oz. can tomato sauce
¼ cup ketchup
1 teaspoon sugar
¾ teaspoon dried oregano
One 8-oz. package cream cheese, softened
⅓ cup grated Parmesan cheese

Cook first three ingredients in skillet until meat is lightly browned and onion tender. Stir in next four ingredients. Cover and simmer gently for 10 minutes. Spoon off any excess fat and add the cheese. Heat and stir until cheese melts and is well combined. (If you like a little kick to your dip, you can always add a few shakes of Crystal Hot Sauce!) Keep warm in chafing dish or small slow cooker. Serve with crackers.

# Pecan Olive Dip

**T**his is one of Lori's recipes that we love. When you are throwing a big dinner party, you don't want to have too many appetizers or you spoil appetites, but you want enough to let people know dinner is going to be spectacular!

12 oz. cream cheese (1 large and
   1 small package) softened
1 small jar green olives with pimiento,
   chopped small
1 small can sliced black olives, chopped small
1 small shallot, chopped fine
½ cup salted pecan pieces, chopped fine
Olive juice, to thin if necessary

Mix all the ingredients together well. Add the olive juice if necessary, but you don't want it too mushy. Fold into a pretty bowl and cover with plastic wrap. Chill until ready to serve.

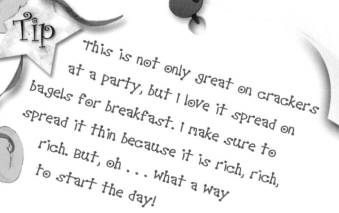

quacky

Tip

This is not only great on crackers at a party, but I love it spread on bagels for breakfast. I make sure to spread it thin because it is rich, rich, rich. But, oh . . . what a way to start the day!

# Bice Bacon Wraps

Bacon (I like Oscar Meyer)
Your favorite breadstick (6 inches long)
  or soda crackers

Preheat oven to 425 degrees. You decide how many bacon wraps you need for your crowd; just make sure that you have the same amount of bacon slices as you do breadsticks. Another alternative is to use soda crackers. But, again, equal parts of each!

Let the bacon sit out until it's room temperature—this makes it much easier to wrap. Don't cut the bacon in half. Use one full piece per breadstick. The best breadsticks to use are the regular, plain old breadsticks (not too thick, not too thin).

Using one piece of bacon per breadstick, start at the bottom of the breadstick and wrap the breadstick with the bacon, covering as much as possible. Continue corkscrewing the bacon around the breadstick.

Lay the bacon wraps on a jelly roll pan, close together, but don't use a rack: They need to cook in the grease to get the flavor.

Bake at 425 degrees until they are crispy, turning once along the way. Make sure and watch them, because they cook quickly! When they are done, lay them out on paper towel to drain.

I make these ahead of time and
then freeze them. They last for
months in the freezer and are great
for quick serving. All you have to do
is take them out and reheat.

# Chipped
# "Where's the Beef?" Dip

## Makes 16 servings

Two 8-oz. packages of cream cheese
4 tablespoons milk
4 jars chipped beef, chopped
1/4 cup onion, finely chopped
1/4 teaspoon pepper
1 cup sour cream
1 green pepper, finely chopped

Preheat oven to 350 degrees. Mix cream cheese,
milk, chipped beef, onion and pepper together. Fold
in sour cream. Spoon into a 1-quart casserole. Bake
for 20 minutes. Serve warm with party rye.

# English Muffin Cheddar Bites

## Makes 24 appetizers

These have been a family favorite for as long as I can remember. They are very rich, but even so, I bet you can't eat just one.

> 6 English muffins, split
> 2 cups cheddar cheese, grated
> ¼ cup onion, chopped
> ½ cup Hellmann's mayonnaise

Preheat oven to 425 degrees. Scoop out muffins. Combine cheese, onion and mayonnaise. Spread on muffin halves. Bake for 15 to 20 minutes till brown and bubbly. May be frozen before cooking . . . just place them on a cookie sheet, freeze, then transfer to a plastic bag and store in the freezer. May be used as needed and cooked without thawing.

quacky Tip

Helping hands need tiny sandwiches! That's why at parties when people are mingling, I like to serve baby sandwiches. This way, there is something for everyone. And they can be made in advance and just heated at serving time!

# What-a-Ham Sandwiches

I like to offer a variety of tiny sandwiches at this party so everyone gets a taste. The nice thing about these is they can be made ahead and simply heated at serving time. Serve them with bread-and-butter pickles.

One 3-pound ham (bake ham the day
    before or buy up a precooked one)
2 sticks butter
8 oz. mustard
24 slices cheddar cheese
12 kaiser rolls, split

Preheat oven to 350 degrees. Cut the ham into roll-sized slices. Mix softened butter with mustard and spread it on the top and bottom of the split rolls. Top the roll halves with the ham slices; lay a slice of cheese on each, then pop them in the oven till cheese is slightly browned and toasted. Serve immediately.

# Tiny Tuna Melts

### Makes 24 Melts

Oh my . . . these are good!

> 4 large cans white albacore tuna
> Mayonnaise of choice (I like Hellmanns)
> 1 large onion, chopped
> Salt and pepper, to taste
> 48 slices cheese
> 2 large, ripe tomatoes
> 12 potato rolls

**M**ix the tuna with just enough mayonnaise to moisten it. Add chopped onion, salt and pepper and mix well. Cut a small potato roll in half; lay a slice of cheese on the bottom. Put a small scoop of the tuna on top of the cheese; then a slice of nice, ripe tomato; then another piece of cheese over the top. Bake open face until the cheese bubbles and browns a bit—about 10 minutes.

# Baby BLTs

Fry up enough bacon (at least a couple of
   pounds) so you don't run out
Wash and dry 2 heads of lettuce
   and pull it apart by hand
Slice a bunch of tomatoes
   (nice and thin)
Toast an assortment of
   bread (white, rye,
   wheat)
Mayonnaise of choice

Spread mayonnaise
on the toasted bread
and then build your
BLT. Bacon first, then lettuce,
then tomato. Put the top slice of
bread on and cut in a cross pattern leaving 4 tiny BLTs. These are
so cute! You need to make sure you are
using a very sharp knife when you cut the
sandwiches so they don't tear apart.

## The Hostess With the Mostest

You've planned and prepped without breaking a sweat. . . . You've cooked, decorated and dimmed the lights. The music is ready, champagne's chilled and the guests are due any minute. You're in a celebratory mood and a festive outfit to match—maybe a Quack sweater? Remember, always dress for a party in something that will fuel conversation: lots of sparkle and eye-popping color.

Take some special time at the beginning of the party to put all your company at ease. Stay near the front door while company is arriving so no one walks in and feels like a wallflower. Next, get something to drink in their hands! Now they feel they have arrived. Introduce them to the people they don't know. Try to be prepared with something they have in common. This gets them chatting very easily and they become best friends right away.

Rescue people who get stuck with a group of people who are boring them. Make sure they know where the food is, the phone is and, most of all, where the bathroom is. Now they are on their own. If they don't have a good time and lots of fun, it's their own fault.

However, not everyone who isn't swinging from the chandeliers and laughing at the top of their lungs is a party pooper. Let me tell you about my husband. He always said each party needs a good listener, and that was him! Butchie would walk into a party and plunk himself down in a chair in the farthest corner of the room. It used to make me crazy. Before we'd go in, and all the way over in the car, I would lecture him to just wander around so it looked like he was mixing in. He didn't have to talk to anyone, just look like he was having a ball. So, on those nights, he would just stay attached to me at the hip, which would irritate me more than having him sit in the corner. I finally learned to let him have fun his way. Not everyone sitting in the corner is a wallflower or a party pooper—they're just having fun in their own way.

When I finally let go of telling Butch how to enjoy the party, he would settle into the corner by himself, but soon a small crowd would be around him. My husband was a great joke-teller, but very quiet about it. People loved to listen to him. He had a great mind and often got the whole group into a very heated and fun discussion about what was going on in the world. Often people would come over to me and say that my husband made the party so special for them. They hadn't wanted to come but were really glad they did.

Sometimes if we just let the world run itself, the best things will unfold. This goes for parties . . . and life. So go with the flow and have fun.

quacky

Tip   Want perfect Christmas light coverage? Try Butchie's famous squint test. The first time I saw Butch doing this, I thought he was crazy, but it really, really works! After you have hung all the lights on your Christmas tree, stand back and look at the tree through squinted eyes. The lights will become all blurred so you can see if you've missed any spots because there will be big dark places. Try it!

# So Many Cookies, So Little Time: A Cookie Exchange

Over the years I have given and gone to many Christmas parties, but my best memories are made during two special things I do at Christmas: my annual cookie exchange and Christmas caroling with my friends.

Just about everyone loves a cookie exchange, even if they don't have a sweet tooth. You get a chance to visit with friends, and when you leave the party, all of your Christmas baking is done. I attended my first cookie exchange in college. My girlfriends and I stayed up into the night, sharing stories . . . and calories! I decided this would be a wonderful get-together to continue after I got married and had my own circle of friends. It took me a few years after getting married, finishing college and settling into my new life as a wife and mother before I remembered the idea again.

The "Cookie Exchange Epiphany" came one Christmas when I had been baking cookies, candies and sweetbreads each night for more than a week. At the end of the marathon bake-off, I stood in my kitchen, my headband covered in flour, knee-deep in sprinkles and colored sugar, too tired to even pour a glass of Mogen David wine. I dusted off the flour and made myself another promise: Next year, a cookie exchange! After all, I always ended up throwing out half of what I'd created when the guilties set in after the holidays.

The first year I invited eight friends, who all showed up carrying the eight dozen cookies I had asked for. Unfortunately, everybody brought the same kind of cookie: peanut butter with a Hershey's Kiss on top! By the end of the night, we were all suffering from chocolate-and-peanut-butter overload (if there is such a thing).

If you want to share some good times with your best friends this season, here's how.

Picking the date is the most important detail. I like to have the party the week after Thanksgiving, before all the other holiday parties start.

*quacky*
**Tip**

When hitting all those flea markets and garage sales in the summer, keep your eyes peeled for cute plates and platters to display your cookies on——red, green or gold plates are especially festive!

# Starting a Sweet
## Tradition of Your Own

Hosting the party before Thanksgiving seems to rush people through their turkey and stuffing. I've hosted the party at night (can you say "sugar-induced insomnia"?), and I've done it on the weekend. Sunday afternoon is my favorite time because the guys are watching football and the gals love to get away.

I like to send out a cute "save the date" postcard on July 25 (Christmas in July). An early invite gets people excited and gives your busy friends a chance to reserve the day early.

You are invited to a

**Cookie**

exchange party

Save the date!
Sunday, November 30th
at Jeanne's House

Bring Cookies

NO Calories

## Make Your Invite Inviting

To plan your own cookie exchange, invite each guest to bring a dozen cookies for each friend who's invited plus one more to eat on the day of the exchange. (Yes, you read that right: a dozen for each person invited, plus one.)

If you're feeling very inspired, you can make your invitations out of an actual cookie. Simply buy some prepackaged dough and use your artistic skills to cut out a big Christmas tree or gingerbread cookie. Poke a hole at the top of the cookie and bake it per the directions on the package. Once the cookie has cooled, frost it. If you have the patience of a saint, write the party details on the cookie with a tube of gel frosting. Remember, I have the patience of a gnat, so I just write "Cookie Exchange" on the cookie, put a string through the hole and attach my paper invitation with the party details. How patient are you? If the answer is "not very," you can just do it my way!

I also ask my guests to bring recipe cards of their creations for everyone attending. Before the age of computers this used to be a lot of work, but today it's a snap. Everyone also brings along a Christmas memory to share. We spend time enjoying each other's company, and everyone gets to tell their favorite holiday story.

## RSVPs

When people RSVP—and you really need them to RSVP—they need to tell you two very important pieces of information: *if* they are going to make it and *what* they're going to make. My first couple of cookie exchange parties, I made the mistake of not asking what people were bringing; although we had fun with all the same cookies, having fun is not the sole purpose of the party. To keep track of who's bringing what, keep a cookie list by the phone. (See recipes starting on page 71 for some great baking ideas if someone can't think of what to make.)

By knowing what cookies you're getting in advance, you can create signs to put by each batch of cookies with the name of the person who made them and what they are. That way, everyone knows who did what (or who didn't have time to bake and ran to the store instead)!

I don't like my guests to leave empty-handed, so everyone gets a present. I fill a huge basket with cute gifts: cookbooks, new rolling pins, baking flour in a decorative glass jar, heart-shaped measuring spoons and cups, cookie cutters and big packages of sparkles and sugars for decorating. Everyone draws a number from a basket when they arrive, and they get to find their gift using the number. This way, I send them home with creative thoughts of sugarplum fairies.

quacky

Tip

For an inexpensive but practical gift, give each guest a couple of rolls of cellophane with a note,

"Let this jump-start your creativity——Happy Baking!"

## The Cookie-Cutter Tree:
## The Center-Pièce de Résistance

For a great centerpiece that really sets the mood, I decorate a table tree with old cookie cutters I pick up at garage sales, flea markets and thrift shops throughout the year. I tie each cutter with a red gingham ribbon and then hang it on the tree. As my friends leave the party, they pick their favorite cookie cutter and take it, along with the cookie recipes from the other guests, as a token of our special time together. And, of course, they're also taking with them dozens of delicious, "made-with-love" Christmas cookies.

Want a centerpiece good enough
to eat? Then make a cookie wreath for
nibbling on during the party. It's simple:
Just arrange an assortment of cookies around
a big round platter and add a red bow.

Cookies given
with love are
always
calorie-free!

Jeanne

# The Cookie Exchange

## LUNCH MENU

MaryAnn's Broccoli Dip

Jeanne's Shrimp Salad

Clover Leaf Rolls

Candy Cane Martini

Peppermint Patty

Coffee Ice Cream Punch

# MaryAnn's Broccoli Dip

## Makes 3 cups

My friend MaryAnn always made the best appetizers and dips. This is one of my favorites. You might be thinking that broccoli is way too healthy to serve at a party, but trust me . . . this is fabulous!

One 10-oz. can cream of mushroom soup
One 10-oz. package frozen chopped
    uncooked broccoli
One 6-oz. package Kraft garlic cheese
    or Velveeta cheese
Garlic powder to taste

Heat soup and then add the chopped broccoli and cheese. Heat until well mixed and then transfer to chafing dish or slow cooker to keep warm. Serve with big Fritos.

**Quacky Tip**

I substitute the garlic cheese for the Velveeta every time. But you can experiment and make this recipe your own with your favorite cheese.

# Jeanne's Shrimp Salad . . .

## Makes 10–12 servings

This is the way the recipe was given to me, and I'm passing it on the same way. Half of the fun is tasting it until you get it just perfect. My kids are the best tasters. They acquired a great palate by doing this!

1 large bag of corkscrew noodles
3 pounds large cooked shrimp, tails off
10 cans of medium deveined shrimp
   (I like Orlean's brand)
1 pint Hellmann's mayonnaise
1 pint Miracle Whip
1 pint sour cream
Sugar, to taste (about a teaspoon)
Salt, to taste
Pepper, to taste
1 large green or yellow onion, chopped
1 envelope Good Seasons Italian Dressing Mix
Mustard sauce (optional)
Cocktail sauce (optional)

Cook the noodles until they are firm, a little longer than al dente. While the noodles are cooking, open the cans of shrimp and drain in a colander.

In a medium bowl, mix together the Hellmann's mayonnaise, Miracle Whip and sour cream, reserving about 3 tablespoons of the mixture for just prior to serving.

# (plus a few big shrimp on the side!)

Add a dab of sugar to pique the flavors; add salt and pepper to taste. To this, add sparingly a few sprinkles of the Good Seasons Italian Dressing Mix. Remember, you can always add more, but it's really impossible to take it out if you overdo it!

When the noodles are done, drain them and rinse with warm tap water. The noodles should be warm when you add the mayonnaise mixture because it will add a richer flavor. Put the noodles in a very large bowl. (I use a large roasting pan so I have enough room to mix well.) Sprinkle half of the chopped onion over noodles, and then start adding the mayonnaise mixture until the noodles are well covered. Add the shrimp and the remaining onion; mix well. Now taste. If you prepare the salad the day before you're serving it, the flavors will deepen. If you're making and serving it the same day, it should taste exactly like you want it to taste.

When you're satisfied with the flavor, add the leftover mayonnaise mixture and toss. The final salad should be the consistency of potato salad. If you make it a day ahead, the sauce will soak into the noodles, so you will have to add more sauce before serving. This recipe is so good and really worth it. You will get so much praise from the crowd.

When it comes time to serve it, I like to dibble-dabble a little mustard sauce and cocktail sauce over the top of mine. Serve with a bed of salad greens or tomato wedges.

# Clover Leaf Rolls

Norton's Restaurant on Green Lake in Wisconsin made THE BEST clover leaf rolls anywhere! My family and I (as well as anyone from that part of the Midwest) will always have fond memories of Norton's.

Start with frozen dough. Let the dough soften and then roll into small balls. Roll each ball in softened butter. Put three balls together in a single section of a buttered muffin tin. Repeat this until you fill all the sections of the tin; let dough rise. After guests arrive, bake the rolls in a pre-heated 400-degree oven for 10 to 12 minutes. The rolls are done when you can take your finger and "tap, tap, tap" on the rolls and they're firm but not burnt.

Your house will smell like the best bakery in town. Serve the rolls piping hot with fresh whipped butter.

# Chocolate Nut Squares

## Makes about 30 squares

1½ sticks Parkay spread (¾ cup)
¾ cup granulated sugar
1¼ cups flour
2 tablespoons heavy cream
1¾ cups pecans or walnuts, coarsely chopped
1 cup flaked coconut
4 ounces semi-sweet chocolate, coarsely chopped

Beat ½ cup of the Parkay and ¼ cup sugar until creamy. Blend in flour. Press mixture on the bottom of an ungreased 9 x 9 x 2-inch baking pan. Bake at 350 degrees for 18 minutes or until edges are lightly browned.

Heat ½ cup sugar, ¼ spread and heavy cream in saucepan, stirring until spread melts and mixture is blended. Stir in pecans and set aside.

Sprinkle coconut and chocolate over the crust. Top with pecan mixture. Bake for 20 minutes more or until golden. Cool and cut into squares.

100% Yummy

# Coconut Macaroons

## Makes 36 macaroons

I love these. We make them in the shape of a heart.

2½ cups shredded sweetened coconut
½ cup sugar
2 tablespoons flour
2 egg whites
½ teaspoon vanilla extract
¼ teaspoon salt

Preheat oven to 350 degrees. Toss 2½ cups of shredded sweetened coconut, ½ cup sugar and 2 tablespoons flour together in a large bowl and set aside. Whisk 2 egg whites, ½ teaspoon vanilla extract and ¼ teaspoon salt together until soft peaks form and then stir in the coconut mixture. Spread heaping tablespoons of the batter into 2-inch heart shapes, 1 inch apart on a parchment-lined baking pan. Bake until macaroons begin to brown around the edges, about 12 minutes.

If you want a real treat, sandwich between two macaroons a filling of raspberry preserves, peanut butter or hazelnut spread. Yum.

# Peanut Butter Bon-Bons

These are really good!

½ cup butter
2 cups crunchy peanut butter
1 box powdered sugar
3 cups Rice Krispies
6 oz. package chocolate chips
1 bar of paraffin
Wax paper

Soften butter and then mix the first 4 ingredients with your hands. Roll the mixture into bite-sized balls and place them on wax paper. Chill. In a double boiler, melt one 6-ounce package of chocolate chips and ½ a bar of paraffin. Dip balls one at a time and place back on wax paper. These bon-bons keep very well (if there's any left!).

# Eve LaTulipe's "Lickety Lips" Chocolate Chip Cookies

## Makes about 2 dozen cookies

In my opinion, this recipe is "The BEST Chocolate Chip Recipe in the World!" Sorry, Mrs. Fields. These cookies are big-hearted and beautiful, just like the ladies who bake and love them. They cause panic attacks, withdrawal tremors, stampedes and personality changes!

These cookies never stay home. They go to visit the grandkids. They are taken to football, baseball, basketball and soccer games. They fish. They go to family reunions and church potlucks. They go scouting. They go to cookie exchanges. They go to funerals. They go on road trips. They appear on people's desks as thank-you gifts. They go to military mailboxes. And they go Federal Express!

4 ½ cups flour (save ¼ cup for the nuts)

2 teaspoons baking soda

1 teaspoon salt

1 cup softened butter

1 cup Crisco shortening (I use one of the
     white Crisco baking sticks)

1 ½ cups white sugar

1 ½ cups light brown sugar

4 eggs

2 tablespoons Mexican vanilla or any dark vanilla
     (i.e., McCormick's, Adams, etc.)

2 cups nuts, very coarsely chopped (Stir ¼ cup flour through the nuts to keep the nuts buoyant in the dough.)
One 12-oz. bag Nestlé real milk chocolate chips

Sift 4 cups of flour, the baking soda and salt together; set aside. In a large mixing bowl, place butter, shortening, sugars, eggs and vanilla, and mix on low until blended. Put mixer on high for 3 minutes. Gradually combine flour/soda/salt mixture into the butter/sugar/egg mix. With a large spoon, alternately add chocolate chips and nuts.

Refrigerate the dough in plastic wrap for at least 2 hours; overnight is best. To bake, use an ungreased cookie sheet (use a flat cookie or jelly-roll pan, not air cushioned). Place 6 gobs of dough on the pan, about ⅓ to ½ cups in size (palm size). Don't compress or mash them; leave them scooped in free form.

Bake immediately at 375 degrees, one pan at a time on the middle oven rack for about 9 to 10 minutes. Bake until cookies are brown, but slightly undercooked in the center. When taken from the oven, let cookies sit on the baking sheet for a minute to hold their form. Carefully transfer to wire baking rack to cool.

Repeat baking with remaining dough, refrigerating bowl between pans. Makes about 2 to 2½ dozen cookies (depending on how much dough you eat yourself).

# Melt-in-Your-Mouth Cookies

### Makes 26 (1-inch) balls

Peanut butter and chocolate lovers rejoice! These cookies are awesome.

1½ cups all-purpose flour
½ cup unsweetened cocoa
½ teaspoon baking soda
¼ teaspoon salt
½ cup granulated sugar (plus more for dipping)
½ cup firmly packed brown sugar
½ cup unsalted butter, softened
1 cup creamy peanut butter, divided
1 teaspoon vanilla extract
1 large egg
¾ cup powdered sugar

Preheat oven to 375 degrees. Whisk together first 4 ingredients in a medium-size mixing bowl. In a separate bowl, beat together granulated and brown sugars, butter, and ¼ cup peanut butter until light and fluffy. Add vanilla and egg, beating to combine. Stir in dry ingredients, blending well. Set dough aside.

Stir together remaining ¾ cup peanut butter and powdered sugar until smooth. With floured hands, roll mixture into 26 (1-inch) balls.

Break off about 1 tablespoon cookie dough; make an indentation in the center with thumb and press 1 peanut butter ball into indentation. Wrap dough over filling, pressing to seal; roll cookie to smooth it out. Repeat for each cookie.

Dip top of each cookie in granulated sugar, then place cookies 2 inches apart on lightly greased baking sheets. Use the greased bottom of a drinking glass to flatten each cookie to about ½-inch thick.

Bake cookies at 375 degrees for 7 to 9 minutes or until set. Let cool on wire rack. Makes 36 cookies.

## Butterscotch Bars

### Makes 2 dozen

18½ oz. package butter pecan cake mix
½ cup softened butter
1 egg
12½ oz. jar caramel topping

reheat oven to 350 degrees. Combine dry cake mix, butter and egg; mix well. Press half of mixture into the bottom of an ungreased 13 x 9-inch baking pan. Bake for 10 minutes. Pour caramel topping over baked crust; sprinkle with reserved cake mixture. Bake an additional 20 to 25 minutes at 350 degrees until lightly golden; cool completely. Cut into bars.

# My Mom's Pineapple Diamonds

## Makes 70 diamonds

1 pound butter or
   margarine
4 cups flour
1 cup sour cream
1 teaspoon vanilla

3 cups drained crushed
   pineapple
1 cup sugar
3 tablespoons cornstarch
Confectioner's sugar

Cut butter into flour with pastry blender. Add sour cream and vanilla. Mix well. Refrigerate dough for 2 hours or overnight. Cook pineapple, sugar and cornstarch over medium heat. Stir the mixture constantly, until thick and clear. Preheat oven to 325 degrees. Roll out $\frac{1}{2}$ of the dough and place in bottom of ungreased jelly-roll pan. Spread cooled pineapple filling over dough and top with rest of dough. Bake for 55 minutes or until golden brown. Sprinkle with confectioner's sugar. Cut into 70 diamonds and refrigerate.

## Vanilla Glaze

$\frac{3}{4}$ cup sugar
$\frac{1}{4}$ cup evaporated milk
$\frac{1}{2}$ cup margarine
1 teaspoon vanilla extract

Mix all ingredients together and bring to a boil. Cook for 30 seconds.

# Candy Cane Cookies

### Makes 2½ dozen

1 cup sugar
⅔ cup margarine, softened
½ cup egg substitute
2 teaspoons vanilla extract
1 teaspoon almond extract
3 cups all-purpose flour
1 teaspoon baking powder
½ teaspoon food coloring

Preheat oven to 350 degrees. Beat together sugar and margarine until creamy, using an electric mixer at medium speed. Beat in egg substitute and extracts; set aside. Mix flour and baking powder; stir into margarine mixture. Divide dough in halves; tint one half with food coloring. Wrap separately; refrigerate for 2 hours. Divide each ball of dough into 32 pieces. Roll each piece into a 5-inch rope. Twist together one red and one plain rope and bend end to form candy canes. Place on ungreased baking sheets. Bake for 8 to 10 minutes until golden. Remove from baking sheets; cool on wire racks. Store in an airtight container.

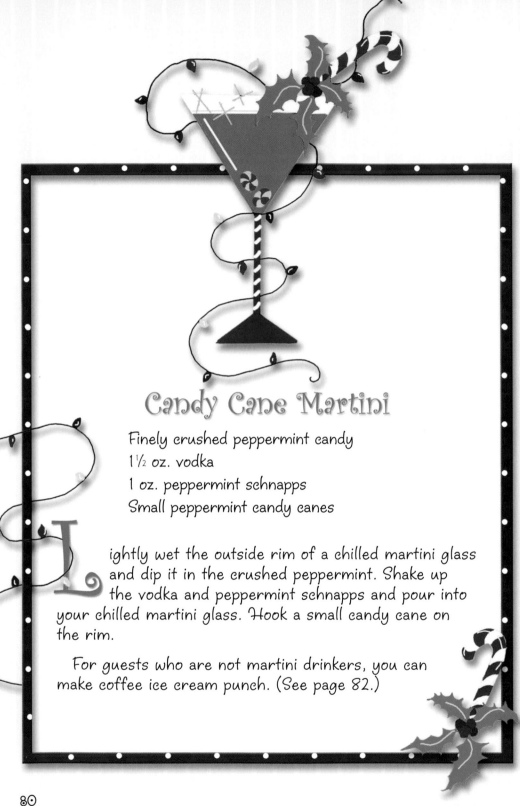

# Candy Cane Martini

Finely crushed peppermint candy
1½ oz. vodka
1 oz. peppermint schnapps
Small peppermint candy canes

Lightly wet the outside rim of a chilled martini glass and dip it in the crushed peppermint. Shake up the vodka and peppermint schnapps and pour into your chilled martini glass. Hook a small candy cane on the rim.

For guests who are not martini drinkers, you can make coffee ice cream punch. (See page 82.)

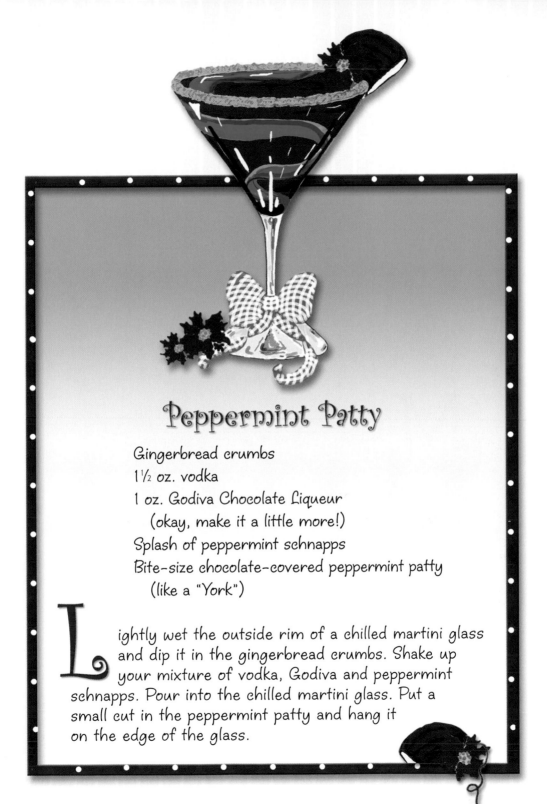

# Peppermint Patty

Gingerbread crumbs
1½ oz. vodka
1 oz. Godiva Chocolate Liqueur
   (okay, make it a little more!)
Splash of peppermint schnapps
Bite-size chocolate-covered peppermint patty
   (like a "York")

Lightly wet the outside rim of a chilled martini glass and dip it in the gingerbread crumbs. Shake up your mixture of vodka, Godiva and peppermint schnapps. Pour into the chilled martini glass. Put a small cut in the peppermint patty and hang it on the edge of the glass.

# Coffee Ice Cream Punch

3 cups strong coffee (cooled)
1 gallon vanilla ice cream
1 pint whipped cream

Mix all ingredients together just before serving. This is a great "women's get-together" punch!

# Five Golden Rings

**W**hen my son Tim got married to Karin, we were so blessed to get a whole bunch of new family to add to our own. As you all know after living through it your-selves, not all in-laws like each other. Well, Karin's maiden name is Graham, so we got the "whole damn Graham family" (as we've come to call them) and we love them all.

The first year Tim and Karin were married, they tried doing Karin's family Christmas and our family Christmas all on the same day. What I've learned is that being pulled in too many directions during the holiday just adds lots of stress to the day, and by the time it's over, everyone is bickering and even I become the wicked mother-in-law. Not wanting to spend our holidays in a tizzy, I made the suggestion that we all just celebrate together when it's most convenient.

Now Tim and Karin get together with her family for a Christmas brunch and to exchange gifts. We've chosen to have our family Christmas gift exchange with them a few days later. It's my biggest stress reliever of all. Plus, it gives me two or three more shopping days, and I get all the sales. I love it!

On Christmas Day, around midafternoon, we all go over to Tim and Karin's house for our blended family holiday. Years ago, Karin's dad, Jack, introduced one of his family traditions to my family, and we've made it a tradition for every Christmas since. Here's what you do:

A few days before Christmas, cut up twelve small pieces of paper and write the verses of the *Twelve Days of Christmas* on them. Fold them in half and put them into a small basket. Then everyone draws their verse from the basket and you sing the song together with everyone soloing on their day. If the crowd is too large, you can pair people up on the verses. It might take some coaxing, but make sure even the shy ones play along. It becomes very, very funny and it's different every year.

On Christmas day, Karin's brother Scott, who plays the piano beautifully, will lead us in a few Christmas carols, then we pass out the verses. The first year we did this, I drew "five golden rings." I had everyone at my house that year, and I was in the middle of gravy-making when they started the song. Well, when they got to me, I would stick my head out of the kitchen, flour dripping from my nose, and at the top of my nanny-goat vibrato, belt out "five golden rings" . . . very loud and very slow. Each time I sang, it brought a laugh. Then everyone joined in for the rest of the verse. From that point on I've always maneuvered it so I got the "five golden rings." However, Karin's brother-in-law, Matt, wants to be the golden-ringer too. He's my competition. Sometimes he tries to steal my draw. He has been known to bribe the "hand-er-outer." He's a sneaky little devil, but I usually survive 'cuz I'm a pushy broad and more sneaky than him! I love to come out on top. . . . Don't try to outsmart the Head Quack. Yes, even on Christmas I might just cheat a little to win.

## Quack Smile

Include the world in your Christmas.
No one should sit home
alone on that day.
What's one or two more
at your table?
Open up your heart and home
and fill all the chairs.
Keep singing and sharing.

## A-Caroling We Will Go

Organizing a caroling party is a fun way to spread the joy at Christmas time.

When I was a young housewife, we didn't have a lot of money, but we had a lot of desire to have fun. We liked to figure out ways to have a party where everyone chipped in. In fact, often we had more fun planning our parties than going to them! Because a caroling party is an "everyone party," we'd have to meet for coffee to plan it. Then we'd meet again to replan and then again to check on everyone's plans. The kids and the dogs would play under the kitchen table while we sat around and coffee'd and planned.

Plus, while we were all together, we solved each other's problems. Discipline problems with a child or two, how to get your husband to take out the trash with no grumbling, whether to take out the kids' tonsils or not. We always left these coffees feeling we were better wives and mothers. Girlfriends make life fun to live. With all this planning, we ended up having three mini parties while planning the big day!

You might say, "I can't do that. . . . I have a job." I had a job, but we'd meet early, before the kids went off to wherever they were off to. We'd start our days together or we'd meet on Saturday and Sunday or evenings. You need to take girlfriend and party-planning time. If we don't find the joy and giggle in life each day, we will sink. Getting together with girlfriends gives us the strength to face the day-to-day workloads.

I believe this is why so many people feel life is so stressed out these days. They forget playtimes. It's like going to school each day and there's no recess! Make time for fun at

Christmas and all year. Here are some ideas for a caroling party that both Lee, my daughter, and I have done. I hope this sparks your creative juices.

The best caroling party we ever had was traveling dinner when all the food was waiting for us in crock-pots! This way everyone could leave their homes and go caroling and share courses in other people's homes. You didn't have to worry about your turn because everything was premade and ready when you finally got to your house!

*First Course:* Eggnog and drinks
*Second Course:* Appetizers
*Third Course:* Soup
*Fourth Course:* Dinner
*Fifth Course:* Dessert
*Sixth Course:* Coffee & hot chocolate

Remember, everything has to be done in a slow cooker. It's fun to find new recipes to make in them.

On a cold, crisp Wisconsin evening, a few weeks before Christmas, we'd all hop into our station wagons with big thermoses of good warm Christmas wassail, leaving the back gate down so a few more could jam in. Then it was off to the first neighborhood to share our joyful songs. We would carol for our friend's neighbors, then hop on over to our friend's house for the first course of our traveling dinner.

Oh, it felt so good to walk into a warm house. We'd "oooh" and "ahhh" at all the decorations, put our feet up for a few moments and get warmed by the fireplace. Our spirits were already warmed by sharing this evening with good friends. Just as we got toasty, snugly warm, it was time to go back out into the cold night. But, as you looked up, you just knew God had joined the party. He had all of his stars twinkling overhead to add to our merriment. We spent the night singing, laughing and spreading Christmas cheer.

When my daughter moved to Florida, she and her husband moved to a great little gated community. Even though they could walk from house to house because they were all on the same few blocks, they chose to move around the neighborhood in a parade of golf carts—it's the Florida way! They decorated each cart in a different motif; some even had Christmas lights on them.

But their group took caroling to a whole new level: They added music. Each of them was given a kazoo and together they formed the "St. Lucie Kazoo Band." Not everyone knows the words to every Christmas carol, but anyone can kazoo.

A Caroling we will go . . .
Travel with us from home to home spreading joy wherever we roam . . .

Make something yummy for us to eat each house a brand new treat!

Your course will be:

Date:          Time:

Starting point:

R.S.V.P.

One year Lee and Mike invited me to come along with them, and all I could think of was my good friend Jerry Long. Jerry never knew the words to any of the songs past "Jingle Bells." So, when we sang "Silver Bells," he just tinkled. He soon found places where he could tinkle in all of the Christmas carols. And he was the greatest at "fa-la-la-ing!" Well, he would have been our best "kazooer." Isn't it fun when your kids take one of your ideas and make it better?

The best thing about my daughter's party? The warm climate. Snow and cold does take some of the joy out of singing, what with your teeth chattering and all! Ah, Christmas . . . it's the perfect time to open your heart and home. Remember, the joy you give to others is the joy that comes back to you all year long. Happy singing. Don't forget to keep humming.

# A-Caroling-We-Will-Go

## MENU

Cider in a Slow Cooker

Donna's Hot Chocolate

I-Bet-You'll-Be-Double-Dipping
Reuben Dip

Artichoke Dip

Potato-Leek Soup

Wisconsin Cheddar Beer Soup

Macaroni & Cheese

Italian Sausage Bake

Beef Stew

Rice Pudding

Crock-Pot Chocolate Fondue

# Cider in a Slow Cooker

## Makes about 8 cups

This will warm you up from the tip of your toes to the tip of your nose.

2 cinnamon sticks
1 teaspoon whole clove
1 teaspoon allspice
8 cups apple cider
½ cup packed brown sugar
1 sliced orange

Put cinnamon, cloves and allspice in a piece of cheesecloth and tie to form a bag.

Warm cider and brown sugar in the slow cooker until the sugar is dissolved. Add the spice bag and place the oranges on the top. Turn the slow cooker on low and simmer for at least 2 hours. . . . Just remove the spice bag before you serve. This recipe makes about 8 full cups, but is easily doubled or tripled!

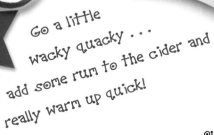

quacky Tip

Go a little wacky quacky . . . add some rum to the cider and really warm up quick!

# Donna's Hot Chocolate

**W**hen my kids were younger, Butchie and I would take them to northern Michigan to go skiing. Well . . . they went skiing, and I became a champion chalet sitter. When the temperature is 38 below, you can bet it's even cold in the chalet. I've found that a Bailey's Irish Cream shield is the best defense against the biting wind! So add a little Bailey's or peppermint schnapps to your hot chocolate and chase away the chillies!

1 box instant powdered milk (8-quart size)
1 pound box Nestle's Quik
One 6-oz. jar non-dairy creamer
½ cup powdered sugar

Mix dry ingredients and put in a container until you need it. The great thing about this is that it can be made way in advance!

To use, add ¼ to ⅓ cup of dry mix per cup of water in your slow cooker and mix it up well. Turn the slow cooker to low, and let it simmer while you are out singing. When you're ready to serve, add whipped cream and enjoy. It doesn't get any better than this!

# I-Bet-You'll-Be-Double-Dipping Reuben Dip

**I**f you are a fan of Reuben sandwiches, you are going to love, love, love this dip! Our friend, Lori, loves to cook, and this is one of her favorite appetizers to serve. She'd tell you that even if you aren't a fan of Reuben sandwiches, you won't be able to resist!

1 ½ pounds thin sliced corned beef
(I get it at the deli)
½ pound grated Swiss cheese
¼ pound grated mild cheddar cheese
1 can sauerkraut
¼ cup Hellmann's mayonnaise
(or Miracle Whip if you like it sweeter)
¼ cup thousand island dressing
3 tablespoons sour cream

Mix everything together except the corned beef in a crock pot. Add the corned beef after you've done all the vigorous stirring. Set the temperature to low and let 'er go! This takes about 45 minutes to really melt nice and slow, and will keep on low for hours! Give it a little stir now and then, and serve with cocktail rye bread.

# Artichoke Dip

This is another one of Lori's appetizer recipes. To this day, it's a favorite of mine.

1 can of quartered artichoke hearts
    (in water, not oil)
1 can of sliced black olives
1 small shallot, chopped fine
1 ½ cups grated Parmesan cheese
1 cup Hellmann's mayonnaise

Optional:
Fresh pressed garlic          Precooked spinach,
Chunk crabmeat                    drained well

   In a bowl, mix the artichoke hearts (squeeze all the water out of them), black olives (drained well) and shallot. Add mayo and stir. Add grated Parmesan; stir again. Add any or all of the optional ingredients at this time and stir it up again. If you add a lot of the optional ingredients, you may have to add just a "tidge" more mayo so it's not too dry! (Lori makes the basic recipe for me because I don't like all the extra stuff . . . but it if was up to her, it would always be loaded with all the options!)

   Transfer to a slow cooker and set the temperature to low. Takes about 30 to 45 minutes to heat through. Stir occasionally. Serve with Fritos or Tostitos Scoops. Yummy!

# Potato-Leek Soup

**A** package of frozen corn is a very tasty addition to this already awesome soup. After all, everyone's a little corny sometimes!

4 cups diced potatoes
3 cups sliced leeks (slice 'em thin)
1 bunch of chopped green onions
2 cups chicken broth
5 slices of cooked, crumbled bacon
1 cup evaporated milk
1 cup shredded cheese
   (pick your favorite here)
Salt and pepper

Mix potatoes, leeks, green onions, chicken broth and bacon together in the crock pot and cook on low for 8 hours. About 20 minutes before serving, add evaporated milk and cheese. Mash with a potato masher to thicken right before serving. Add a little warm milk if it's too thick.

# Wisconsin Cheddar Beer Soup

### Makes about 15 large servings

There's nothing better than coming in from the cold to a nice warm bowl of cheddar beer soup. Mmmmm, mmmmm!

1 cup chopped onion
1 cup chopped celery
1 tablespoon butter
1 cup diced carrot
6 cups chicken broth
½ pound grated cheddar cheese
½ cup flour
½ teaspoon dry mustard
½ teaspoon Worcestershire sauce
1 can of your favorite beer

Sauté onion and celery in butter until soft; add carrots until they are just starting to get tender. Pour the beer and the chicken broth into the crock pot. Slowly stir in the flour, dry mustard and Worcestershire sauce so it doesn't get lumpy. Add the sautéed veggies and mix it up. Add the cheese and mix again. Cover and set the temperature on your crock pot to low. It takes about an hour to really heat up and get all melty!

I like to sneak in a box of dry
Campbell's Cream of Chicken Soup mix
(the 4-package box) and an extra can of
beer or two . . . but, that's just me! If I
really want to jazz it up, I'll add leftover mashed potatoes instead of the
flour. Now you can even buy mashed potatoes already mashed. Yoder's are
the best if you are lucky
enough to have them
in your area.

In Wisconsin, cheese-heads
buy their cheese in the shape
of stuff like cows, pigs and
the state of Wisonsin . . . it
tastes so much better!

Jeanne

# Macaroni & Cheese

My friends John and Nancy Furr use macaroni and cheese as an appetizer. They serve it in small cups, and when they bring it out the people cheer! Nancy also uses a smoky cheese. I'm not a real fan of the smoky. . . . There's enough smoky areas in life already, so I don't add it to my cheese!

2 cups prepared elbow macaroni
2 tablespoons oil
12-oz. can evaporated milk
1 ½ cups milk
3 cups pasteurized processed cheese spread, shredded
¼ cup butter, melted

Combine macaroni and oil; toss to coat. Pour into a slow cooker; stir in remaining ingredients. Cover and cook on low setting for 3 to 4 hours, stirring occasionally.

# Italian Sausage Bake

This makes your house smell like you walked into a fine Italian restaurant! That's 'a good!

8 Italian sausages
26-oz. can spaghetti sauce
6-oz. can tomato paste
1 onion, sliced thin
1 tablespoon grated Parmesan cheese
1 teaspoon dried parsley
1 cup water
1 pound spaghetti, precooked
1 teaspoon of garlic (optional)

Simmer the sausages in a water-filled skillet for 10 minutes. Drain and slice them up. Put the sausages in the slow cooker; add spaghetti sauce, tomato paste, onion, Parmesan cheese, parsley, water and garlic if you are using it. Stir it up good and set it on low for 4 hours. About an hour before you are ready to serve, turn the temperature up to high. Serve over spaghetti and sprinkle with fresh grated parmesan cheese. This recipe makes enough for eight, but you can serve many more with this amount if you are serving other things as well.

You can also make this with spicy Italian sausage if you are brave enough!

# Beef Stew

I think beef stew has to be one of the best comfort foods ever!

1 pound beef, cut in chunks
One 16-oz. can tomato paste
1 large onion, chopped
1/4 cup A-1 Steak Sauce
1 teaspoon salt
2 bay leaves

Little dash of red wine
Water as needed
Mixture of vegetables
(I use carrots, potatoes
and mushrooms)

Brown the beef in a hot frying pan and put in the slow cooker. Add the rest of the ingredients and mix well. I'll add a dash of red wine to the stock for a yummy flavor. Make sure there is enough liquid to cover all your meat and veggies.

Turn the slow cooker on the low setting, and let it go for about 6 hours. Stir it once in a while to make sure all the ingredients soak up the juices.

quacky

Tip

When people make beef stew, they tend to cut the veggies too small. Carrots and onions seem to disappear. Cut your veggies in big chunks. Now you've got something to bite into. It's more fun to take a big chunk out of life.

# Rice Pudding

ice pudding reminds me of the good old days. Growing up, it was a special treat and it still brings back fond memories for me. It's the ultimate comfort food on a cold, snowy night. You'll sleep well after just a bit of this!

2 ½ cups cooked rice

1 ½ cups scalded milk

⅔ cup brown sugar

3 eggs, beaten

1 teaspoon salt

2 teaspoons cinnamon

½ teaspoon nutmeg

½ cup raisins

3 tablespoons soft butter

Lightly grease a slow cooker. Pour all ingredients in, and cook on high for up to 2 hours. Turn the slow cooker to low when ready to serve.

# Crock-Pot Chocolate Fondue

1 ½ teaspoons butter or margarine
8 chocolate candy bars (plain or with almonds)
1 ½ cups miniature marshmallows
3 tablespoons milk
½ cup whipping cream
Toothpicks

Grease the inside of the slow cooker with the butter. Place the candy bars, milk and marshmallows in the slow cooker. Cover and turn it on low for about 30 minutes, stirring every now and then.

When it's melted and smooth, slowly and gradually add the whipping cream. Cover and keep warming for up to 4 hours. I love setting this out on a tray with a grand assortment of goodies to dip. You can use angel food cake, bananas, an assortment of berries, green apples or grapes.

quacky Tip

I love potato chips and pretzels to dip—use the big long pretzel rods. Double dipping is allowed! The salty and sweet are soooo good. It's sort of like life ...a little mix of everything!

# Christmas in July

One of the best Christmas parties I've ever gone to was held in July. I had a dear friend who was diagnosed with multiple sclerosis. She was right down in bed on a very fast track to thinking that her life was all over. Finally, her doctor convinced her she did indeed have many good years ahead, but only if she got out of bed and started thinking positively. She needed to enjoy life . . . celebrate it! And so she did. She set out to create a life of celebration.

Since she was in bed at Christmastime and missed all the fun, she and her husband decided to have a Christmas in July party in Green Lake, Wisconsin. They decorated the whole place with huge trees and strung lights all over the place, both inside the house and out.

We came with gifts for everyone and sang carols to all the people on the lake. What made it all so great was her joy. She had taken her "pits" and planted ideas in all of our minds on a new way to celebrate not just Christmas but life itself.

On July 25, have all your friends and family over. It's a stress-free time of the year, and it's so much more fun to decorate in the warm weather!

# Christmas-in-July

## MENU

Don't-Be-Crabby Bisque

Chicken and Wild Rice Casserole

Jeanne's Coleslaw

Fruited Jell-O Mold

Magic Dip

# Don't-Be-Crabby Bisque

This is the best when you have fresh crabmeat! I love to make it and serve with a smattering of grated cheddar.

One 10-oz. can cream of asparagus soup
One 10 ¾-oz. can cream of mushroom soup
1 cup milk
1 cup half & half
½ teaspoon Worcestershire sauce
½ pound crabmeat, picked free of
    broken shells
¼ cup dry sherry

Combine all ingredients in a heavy saucepan and bring to a boil. Reduce heat and simmer for 10 to 15 minutes. Yum! You can keep this in the freezer for up to a month.

# Chicken and Wild Rice Casserole

## Makes 10–12 servings

**M**y kids hated this . . . but, oh, it was one of my favorites! It's great for a big family get-together. You can make it ahead of time and freeze or make two casseroles out of this!

Two 6.2-oz. packages fast-cooking, long grain
   and wild rice mix
¼ cup butter or margarine
4 celery ribs, chopped
2 medium onions, chopped
Two 8-oz. cans sliced water chestnuts, drained
5 cups chopped cooked chicken
4 cups (1 pound) shredded cheddar cheese, divided
Two 10¾-oz. cans cream of mushroom soup, undiluted
One 16-oz. container sour cream
1 cup milk
½ teaspoon salt
½ teaspoon pepper
2 cups soft breadcrumbs (homemade)
One 2.25-oz. package sliced almonds, toasted

Prepare rice mixes according to package directions.

Meanwhile, melt butter in a large skillet over medium heat; add celery and onion. Sauté 10 minutes or until tender.

Combine water chestnuts, cooked rice, celery, onion, chicken, 3 cups cheese and next 5 ingredients in a very large bowl.

Spoon mixture into a lightly greased 15x10-inch baking dish or 4-quart baking dish. Top casserole with breadcrumbs. Bake uncovered at 350 degrees for 35 minutes. Sprinkle with remaining 1 cup cheese and almonds; bake 5 more minutes.

107

# Jeanne's Coleslaw

I've been making this coleslaw for years and it's always been a hit. Lately, my daughter, Lee, has taken to making it. In fact, when my father was very ill, one of his last requests to Lee was for her to make this for him. It's a family tradition. My favorite way to eat this is on a turkey sandwich. Take a leftover roll, cut it in half and lay turkey on it; then pile on the coleslaw. Salt and pepper to taste.

Slaw:

1 large head cabbage—"Slaw it!"
   (or 2 small bags from grocery store)
1 small can pineapple (small chunk) drained
   (keep the juice)
3/4 bag of mini marshmallows (use the rest of the bag
   for hot chocolate . . . the weather's getting nippy!)
Dash of apple vinegar

Sauce:

Cool Whip                 Marzetti Slaw Dressing

In a large mixing bowl, mix the slaw, drained pineapple and mini marshmallows. In a separate bowl, mix up the sauce by adding half a container of Cool Whip and half a bottle of

Marzetti slaw dressing, but just enough to dress the slaw, not to drown it. Add salt and pepper to taste. Add a sprinkle of pineapple juice and drink the rest (in a glass with Malibu rum, it makes a yummy drink!). Add a dash of apple vinegar (you probably won't want to drink the rest of that!).

Make this in the morning or the day before. Leave it a little dry—the pineapple will add juice. About an hour before serving, stir it up! If you like it creamier, just add a bit more Cool Whip and slaw dress-ing. Tastes "oh so good!"

quacky Tip If I need to add more dressing before serving I test and see if it needs some "zing." If so, I'll add a little Miracle Whip to the dressing mix. Taste! Taste! Taste! If you like it, all your guests will, too!

# Fruited Jell-O Mold

## Makes about 10 servings

**M**y friend, Beth Ann, is the best Jell-O mold maker. She has the patience to "putz" with them. She has many, many recipes that she makes, but I asked her for one of her less complicated ones to share!

2 packages strawberry Jell-O (3 oz.)
1½ cups boiling water
2 cups ice cubes
1 package (10 oz.) frozen sliced strawberries
1 can (13½ oz.) crushed pineapple
2 tablespoons lemon juice
Walnuts
1 envelope Dream Whip whipped
   topping mix

Dissolve 1 package gelatin in ¾ cup boiling water. Add 1 cup of ice cubes and stir until it starts to thicken. Remove any of the ice that didn't melt. Stir in lemon juice, pineapple, strawberries and walnuts. Pour into 5-cup mold and chill. This mixture should go about halfway up the mold.

Prepare Dream Whip according to package directions.

Dissolve the last package of Jell-O in ¾ cup
boiling water. Add 1 cup of ice and stir until it
starts to thicken. Again, remove any of the ice
that didn't melt. Fold in the Dream Whip.
Pour into the mold over the fruited layer.
Chill at least another hour before serving.

# Magic Dip

## Makes about 8 servings

You know why I call this magic dip? Because it disappears so fast you'd think it was magic!

1 package (8 oz.) softened cream cheese
1 cup semisweet real chocolate chips
$\frac{1}{2}$ cup coconut, toasted
$\frac{1}{2}$ cup chopped peanuts
Graham crackers

Spread cream cheese onto the bottom of a 9-inch microwavable pie plate or dish. Top with chocolate chips, coconut and peanuts. (Adding some Reese's Pieces on top of this is mighty tasty too!)

Microwave on 50 percent power for 3 minutes or so or until warm (watch out . . . some microwaves cook faster than others). You want it to be just slightly melty. Serve with graham crackers.

# Girlfriends-Only Tea

Years ago I heard a great story that I think about when I'm feeling frazzled. It goes like this:

A young woman went to visit her grandmother. When she got there, the elderly woman asked her if she'd like some tea. "Yes," she replied, because she was feeling very tired and lost in her life.

Her grandmother began pouring the tea, pouring, pouring, pouring, until hot liquid was running over the rim, onto the saucer, and then onto the table. The young woman shouted, "Stop!" And her grandmother said, "Yes, you need to stop. You are like this teacup; so full there is no room inside you for anything new. You are not lost; you are just too full. You need to release your burdens and make room for something new. You need to have room for joy in your life."

I believe this happens to many of us during the holidays. Our lives are so full normally that adding Christmas on top of it sometimes makes us feel like we might explode. What better way to relieve some stress than to invite your girlfriends over? Kick back, relax and let your girlfriends pick you up. The best part of this menu? You can always get pizza delivered instead!

Quack a Smile

Remember your blessings, forget the day's troubles.

# Girlfriends Tea

## MENU

FROM SANTA

Spiced Tea with Milk

Sugar-Nut Brie

Tea Sandwiches with Cucumber

Black Bottom Cupcakes

Velvet Crumb Cake

# Spiced Tea with Milk

Soothing and wonderful . . . that's the only description I can think of for this wonderful tea.

4 ¼ cups water
¼ teaspoon ground clove
1 cinnamon stick
1 tablespoon loose black tea
1 cup hot milk
1 tablespoon sugar (to taste)

Bring water, cloves and cinnamon to a boil. Remove from heat and add tea. Cover and steep for 4 minutes. Strain tea and stir in hot milk and sugar to taste.

I'm not a real fan of strong tea, so I only let it steep for 4 minutes. But, if you like a hearty tea, you can let it steep a few minutes longer.

# Sugar-Nut Brie

## Makes 16–20 servings

This is such an elegant appetizer. It's easy and takes hardly any time to prepare, but my friends think I spent hours making it!

¼ cup packed brown sugar
¼ cup chopped macadamia
    nuts or pecans
1 tablespoon brandy
1 round of brie (14 oz.)

Apple wedges
Pear wedges
Lemon juice
Assorted crackers

In a small bowl stir the sugar, nuts and brandy together. Cover and chill for at least 24 hours or up to a week. At serving time, place the brie on an ovenproof platter or pie plate. Bake at 350 degrees for 4 or 5 minutes or until brie is slightly softened. Spread the sugar mixture in an even layer on top of the warm brie, and bake for 2 or 3 minutes longer or until sugar melts.
Brush the fruit with lemon juice and arrange on one side of the brie. Arrange crackers on the other.

quacky Tip

Experiment with different nuts if you are not a pecan or macadamia fan. Use your imagination!

# Tea Sandwiches with Cucumber

1 or 2 cucumbers
Salt and pepper to taste
White wine vinegar
Whole wheat, rye or pumpernickel bread,
    sliced very thin
Butter, softened

Peel cucumber and slice into nearly transparent slices. Sprinkle slices of cucumber with a smidge of white wine vinegar and salt and pepper. Put them in a colander and let drain for about half an hour. Set them on a paper towel as you take them out of the colander to remove excess moisture.

Lightly butter the slices of bread and cover with two layers of cucumber. Salt and pepper again for taste. Cover with another slice of bread and press firmly down with the palm of your hand. Cover and chill before serving.

To make these look very chichi, I cut off the crusts and either cut them into little triangles or use a round biscuit cutter to shape them into circles. I've occasionally been known to use my ducky cookie cutter too!

# Black Bottom Cupcakes

This is another one of my friend Donna's famous recipes. It always brings me back to happy, carefree times. I love the feeling of relaxation and true friendship this recipe brings. What better time than Christmas to share this with your friends?

Combine:

| | |
|---|---|
| One 8-oz. package cream cheese | 1 unbeaten egg |
| ½ cup sugar | ⅛ teaspoon salt |

Stir in:

1 cup chocolate chips

Then, in another dish, combine:

| | |
|---|---|
| 1½ cups flour | 1 cup sugar |
| ¼ cup cocoa | 1 teaspoon baking soda |
| ½ teaspoon salt | |

Add together to flour mixture, and beat well:

1 cup water
½ cup oil
1 tablespoon vinegar
1 teaspoon vanilla

Fill cups with the second mixture, and top with the cream cheese mixture. Sprinkle with sugar and chopped nuts. Bake at 350 degrees for 30 to 35 minutes.

119

# Velvet Crumb Cake

This is a wonderful crumb cake to have with tea. Treat yourself and your friends. You're worth it!

1 ½ cups original Bisquick
½ cup sugar
1 egg
½ cup milk or water
2 tablespoons shortening
1 teaspoon vanilla
Broiled topping (See below)

Heat oven to 350 degrees. Grease and flour an 8-inch square or 9-inch round pan. Beat all ingredients except topping in a large bowl on low speed for 30 seconds, scraping the bowl constantly. Beat on medium speed for 4 minutes, scraping the bowl occasionally. Pour into pan. Bake 30 to 35 minutes or until toothpick inserted in center comes out clean; cool slightly.

Spread topping over cake. Set oven control to broil. Broil about 3 inches from heat for about 3 minutes or until golden brown.

Broiled Topping:
Mix together ½ cup flaked coconut, ⅓ cup packed brown sugar, ¼ cup chopped nuts, 3 tablespoons margarine or butter and 2 tablespoons milk.

# Part Three

## Deck Your Halls:
## Decorating with Sparkle and Shine

# Flocked Trees and Christmas Fairies

A few years ago I bought an artificial Christmas tree. It was gorgeous and huge and flocked with the most sparkly white snow. Oh, I had wanted a flocked tree forever, but everyone always said not to buy a flocked tree in Florida because it would turn yellow over the years of being stored in a hot attic. But one year I just couldn't stand the gnawing desire so I just went ahead and chanced it . . . pure joy the day it arrived. I was a happy girl! The flocked tree would be my main tree in the front window. All of my ornaments are red and white: Santas, candy canes and gingham ribbon. I knew they would just "pop" on this tree and I couldn't wait to set it up.

Well, after putting all of the ornaments and bows on the tree I stepped back to admire my creation . . . and what I saw made me want to cry (except big girls don't cry over Christmas tree mistakes). All of my ornaments got swallowed up by this huge white tree. *Were my friends right about not buying it?* I just couldn't bear to send it back— besides, I had a hard enough time getting it *in* the house; I wasn't going to attempt to take it back out.

I made myself feel better thinking that maybe it could be a part of my Christmas theme and just not have anything on it. The flocking could be the decoration.

Every time I passed it, it looked like such a lonely stepchild of a tree. *What could I do to help this pitiful tree?* One day Lee came over and had one of those great "lightbulb" ideas and went right to it.

My house is a house full of signs. She started pulling them off the wall and sticking them into the tree. Woman of little faith that I was, I kept saying that her idea was not going to work. She was used to me bah-humbugging her ideas, so she just continued finding red and green signs and tucking them into my poor tree. She was like a whirling dervish, and then as quickly as she started, she was done. She had sparkles in her hair, flocking dripping off her shoulders and my walls were almost signless. She stepped back, studied the tree, and then all of a sudden, she hopped up and down and clapped her hands together. Saying she'd be right back, she bounded up to the attic and returned carrying one of my largest Christmas fairies. Declaring she had found the magic, she

*quacky*

**Tip**

Keep a log of where all your special ornaments have come from so you can pass the stories and memories on to your children, and they to theirs.

123

wrapped the fairy around the top of the tree and put a magic wand in his hand, making it look as though all the Christmas signs came from his wand.

She gave the tree a purpose. And, when she was finished, she flopped down on the chair, brushed off the flocking and sparkles and said her job was done (and, if she did say so herself, she was darn good at her job)! I looked at this sweet daughter of mine and thought that she was just magical. I thank God for her. She brought life to my sad tree, and joy and sparkle to her mom's heart— and that's what Christmas is all about.

Believe . . .

hang it on your wall,

put it on your mirror,

hang it on your tree.

Merry Christmas!

Jeanne

If you are lacking for inspiration, here are some of my favorite ideas for themed trees.

Themed trees are a great place to put your knick-knacks or to place any of your collectibles. The secret is lots of consistent color and lots of stuff.

This is a great tree for Christmas in July

Dream!

I just love gingham—and who couldn't use a little more joy?

Quack, Quack!

Life's just ducky!

This tree is a reminder to make room for what
matters during the holidays.

This is a great tree that can brighten any room. I have roosters all over my house and they make a big hit during the holidays. I like to keep this tree up year-round!

# Hang-on-to-Good-Wishes Tree

Years ago I created what I call a Christmas card tree. A beautiful tree—even a not-so-beautiful tree—can take on a special meaning when heartfelt greetings are hanging from its branches. Plus, it's simple to make.

All you do is punch holes in the cards you receive—even your party invitations. Then you hang the cards from your tree with ribbon (I like red gingham). This is a great tree if you want a second or third tree but don't have anything to hang on it or you are a little short of cash after your Christmas shopping.

A wish tree is also a great place to hang all the Christmas "stuff" the kids bring home from school (You know, the "art" you hang on your refrigerator the rest of the year). When their stuff hangs on the refrigerator, it gets dusty and dirty and often gets thrown away. If you save their art for the wish tree, it makes the kids feel special that their creations get saved, packed away with the Christmas decorations, and then pulled out year after year. You'll even find some kids start making special things for their tree. Then when they go off on their own, you can give them their masterpieces back to start their own wish tree with their kids.

I began this tradition in the early sixties when my kids were very young. Then I found Christmas cards I loved in the drugstores. I even started buying special cards for my tree . . . the more sparkle the better. I especially loved 3-D cards. It got to be a fun project for me when all the Christmas cards went on sale. (January is the best month for holiday decorating people like me.) In the last few years I have moved on to sign and word ornament trees. Try it—you might start a new tradition in your family.

quacky

Tip

If you don't want to do a whole card tree, buy a wreath and attach your cards around it. You get the great smell of fresh greens, the decoration changes each day, and it gives your family and friends something special to look at. Plus, it's overflowing with good wishes!

# Festive Flea-Market Finds

I love, love, love old-fashioned Wisconsin-type flea markets—you can find some great old stuff. Here's what I look for when shopping for decorations dirt-cheap:

- Old sets of children's blocks. Find enough of them to spell out "CHRISTMAS GREETINGS" and tuck them everywhere—on the mantle, in a wreath. Another idea is to screw tiny ring hooks into the blocks and hang from a ribbon on the back of guests' chairs to spell their names. (You might want to invite people with short names, or just use their initials.) I use these blocks all year-round. Put BELIEVE on your desk and see what happens!

- Really old cupcake tins. Fill them with votive candles and set amongst some greens.

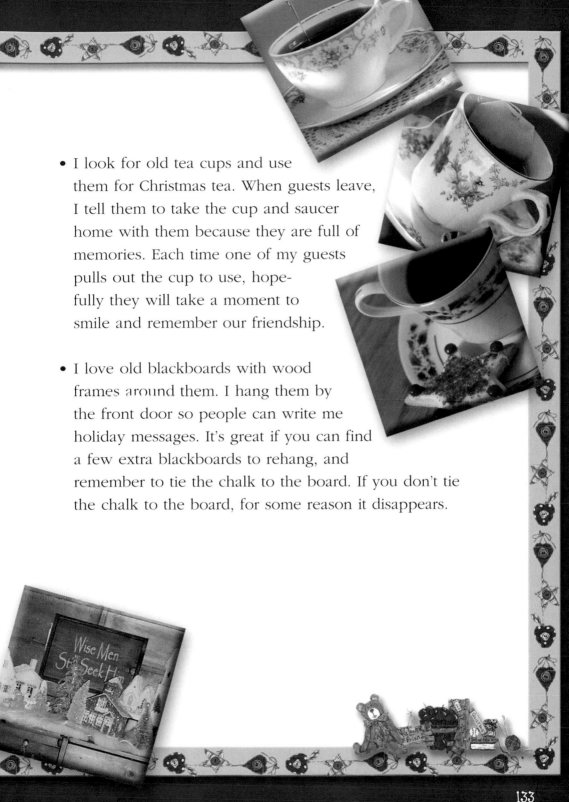

- I look for old tea cups and use them for Christmas tea. When guests leave, I tell them to take the cup and saucer home with them because they are full of memories. Each time one of my guests pulls out the cup to use, hopefully they will take a moment to smile and remember our friendship.

- I love old blackboards with wood frames around them. I hang them by the front door so people can write me holiday messages. It's great if you can find a few extra blackboards to rehang, and remember to tie the chalk to the board. If you don't tie the chalk to the board, for some reason it disappears.

# Quacky Craft Ideas

**1** This season, greet your guests with a cheery holiday greeting. Just bend heavy wire into word shapes—"DREAM", "WISH" or "NOEL". Then attach fresh greenery sprigs to the wire letters with green florist tape. You can either use the greens you cut off your Christmas tree, or, even better, use artificial greens so you'll have the decoration for years. Put a hanger on the back, hang and enjoy.

**2** Buy a bunch of cheap votives at the Dollar Store. Wash them with warm soapy water and dry well. Using craft glue, write seasonal sayings, like "HO, HO, HO" and then sprinkle with glitter. You can also write people's names on the votives and use them for place cards. Your guests can take their candleholders home with them. These are so simple to make and really gorgeous when you use them to hold candles.

**3**
Buy some six-inch or ten-inch pillar candles and write JOY using craft glue and glitter. I'm most likely to use gold or silver glitter, but you could also use red and green. Then wrap a ribbon around the candle under the word and add a brass charm (if you used gold glitter, use a silver charm; if you used silver glitter, use a gold charm). I love these!

**4**
Buy a box of cheap silver or gold round ball ornaments at the Dollar Store. Drizzle the ornaments with craft glue and sprinkle glitter, glitter *(did I say more glitter?)* all over them. I like to put silver glitter on gold ornaments and gold glitter on the silver ones. Believe me, filling a tree with just these ornaments is so easy and your tree will be so elegant.

**5**
Decorate some small clay pots by painting them white and adding glitter to the top lip. You can jazz them up even more by drawing glitter stars or writing words across the top lip. Once they're dry, place votive candles in them and use them to line your driveway. These are so different from the typical paper-bag luminaries and oh so pretty.

# A Candy Cane Bouquet

In the last few years there have been many new, fancy—and expensive—outdoor Christmas decorations. A few years ago I noticed these really great lit candy canes. I loved them, but they were just too pricey for me. Then, one year I got a flyer from one of our discount stores that had these big candy canes for a fraction of the price found in the specialty Christmas shops. Well, I bounded right down there and bought enough of them to go up and down my driveway. I was so thrilled that I had gotten them at such a bargain price.

The next night I went out to dinner with some friends. On the way home I drove around admiring the Christmas decorations in the neighborhood. I quickly spotted a trend. A few years before it had been icicle lights. But this year, to my horror, it was candy cane lights. Apparently all of my neighbors had all gotten the same flyer as I had! Not only had they beaten me to the store, but they were a step ahead of me getting them out.

Everyone's driveway was lined with candy cane lights.

What could I do to keep our neighborhood from looking like a giant Candy Land game gone wrong? It took a couple of days, but I came up with a great idea (if I do say so myself).

I got two really big white pots and arranged some Christmas tree greens in them. Next I added some white lights to the greens and then stuck the candy canes in. I made a huge bouquet of the potted candy canes and set them on both sides of my front and back doors. They greeted all my guests with such fun and sweetness. This is a great idea for anyone who lacks a green thumb.

# Quacky Candy Cane Ideas

**E**very year I put candy canes in bowls around the house because they are so pretty and festive. A lot of my friends who live in the Midwest will keep their candy canes and use them for decorations the following year. But, where I live in Florida, that's just impossible. I'd have a three-ring bug circus if I didn't get rid of them! So, here are a few ideas for fun things to do with candy canes.

1. Candy canes make great stir sticks in your hot beverages.
2. Add crushed candy canes to vanilla frosting. Spread this on graham crackers to make graham cracker peppermint sandwiches! These are *really* good with chocolate graham crackers.
3. Add crushed candy cane to just about any dessert: Melt white chocolate and make candy cane bark; mix them in with your Rice Krispy treats or add a little peppermint zing to your cookie recipes.
4. Dip candy canes in melted chocolate and refrigerate. After they are set, put them out on a pretty tray. The kids love them!

# Candy Cane Fudge

## Makes about 64 pieces

2 packages 10-oz. vanilla baking chips
1 can sweetened condensed milk (14 oz.)
½ teaspoon peppermint extract
1½ cups crushed candy canes
A dash of red or green food coloring

Line an 8-inch square baking pan with aluminum foil. Grease the foil generously.

Combine vanilla chips and sweetened condensed milk in a saucepan over low heat, stirring frequently. Continue to stir until the vanilla chips are almost melted. Remove from heat and keep stirring until the mixture is smooth. When the chips are melted, stir in peppermint extract, food coloring and candy canes.

Spread evenly in the bottom of the pan and chill for 2 hours. Cut into squares.

This recipe can make as many as 64 pieces of fudge, but I like to cut them a bit bigger and get less out of it. I also split up the batch of fudge while it's warm, <u>before</u> I add the food coloring, so I can make some with red food coloring and leave some white. This way, I alternate colors when spreading them on the bottom of the pan so they make a red-and-white striped presentation. When these are cut up and set out on a plate, it's very festive.

# North Pole Peppermint Pie

### Makes 8 servings

While I'm not a fan of chocolate, I am a fan of "easy." This is a great dessert that won't heat up your kitchen—great for parties when you have ten other things on the stove!

⅔ cup butter

1 cup sugar

3 eggs, beaten

Two 1-oz. squares unsweetened chocolate

⅓ cup semi-sweet chocolate chips, melted

One 9-inch premade graham cracker crust (or you can make your own if you're feeling up to it!)

1 cup heavy cream, whipped (or use store-bought whipped cream)

⅓ cup crushed peppermint sticks

Cream the butter and sugar together until they're lightly mixed. Hand-mix in the eggs until blended. Add the chocolate squares and the chocolate chips and mix well. Pour mixture into a graham cracker crust. Refrigerate for 3 to 4 hours. Just before serving, spread whipped cream on top and sprinkle with crushed candy canes.

# Pretty Party Napkins

Over the years I've had all kinds of napkins: really expensive ones from Switzerland, cheap ones from the Dollar Store, nice ones from Pottery Barn. But they all need special care, like spotting to take off lipstick and wine stains; plus they need ironing. And, no matter how well you store them, they need re-ironing when you go to use them. Now, I'm not a good ironer to begin with, much less a re-ironer. So over the years I've taken to using dish towels for napkins. Dish towels come in many designs and great colors, they're very absorbent, very big and don't stain very easily. Best of all, they don't need ironing!

I buy the dish towels that measure about 22" x 14". I love red and white checks, blue and white checks, and the white with red stripes. I like to stencil *"Ho Ho Ho"* on them in red. Then, when the stencil's dry, I press it to set in place. (If you set it right, it will last for years.) My all-time favorite design is to write *"Merry Christmas"* in green on red-and-white gingham.

If you find it's too much to stencil, you can also use paint pens. While the end result will be very pretty, the project can get a little messy because the paint pens take a while to dry. If you're short on time, you can also use silver and gold glitter pens, which don't take so long to dry. I also love using permanent markers because they write easily and dry instantly.

It's important to remember to put something under your project because the ink will often bleed through. You don't want this message stained into your kitchen table for many years to come! I use cardboard, tag board or white butcher paper (I like to use the white butcher paper because it has a wax backing and nothing seeps through). Please don't use newspaper or you will end up with newsprint all over the back of your project . . . and your clothes . . . and your fingers and toes.

Hey, while you have the paint pens out, why not make some funny hand towels for the bathroom? Or how about some Christmas pillow-cases for the beds? It really perks up the bedroom.

Another thing I've started doing as our crowd grows older is to make bibs out of kitchen towels. This is really so easy and can be done by hand. I just sew ribbon to the top of the towel. If you're not a fan of sewing, you can find many fuse and bond products so you can simply put the ribbon on the towel and apply heat. Zap—like magic . . . a bib!

"Eat" Holidays are calorie free!

I'm not big on napkin rings——I'd rather use pretty ribbon, bows and raffia around my napkins. At Christmastime, I like to tie an ornament to each napkin so my guests have something to take home with them. Sometimes I use a big jingle bell, some incense sticks or a big piece of mistletoe.

You can also put the napkins in cute Santa hats. Of course, you can't let your guests get away with not wearing the hat. It gets everyone in the holiday mood!

# 'Twas the Knit Before Christmas

Quacker alert: Closet too full? Here's a quacky idea to help!

One of the things I hear a lot from women is that they have either gained or lost weight so they own sweaters in three different sizes and don't know what to do with them. Well, one option is to give their sweaters to friends so they can also enjoy the feeling of a great Quacker sweater. Or, they can use some of my fun ways to turn Quack sweaters into great gifts or fun decorations around the house. Here's how:

I took one of my cardigan sweaters that had feathers around the collar and cut it into a Christmas stocking (the feathers were the top of the stocking). Not one for detail myself, I used one of my kids' Christmas stockings for a pattern. If you're a person who needs more exact instructions, you can go to the fabric store and buy a pattern. If you have an interlock sewing machine, you can put the two right sides together and zip the two edges together. I don't have a snazzy machine, so I just sewed it all by hand, using some yarn and a big needle. I used the old baseball stitch (looks like CCCC); you know, end over end. Making a stocking this way is easy and fun! Just make sure you sew your stocking really tight so it holds all the booty from Santa!

I've also made Christmas pillows the same way. I cut out the pillow pieces and sew three sides together. Then I turn the pillow right side out and stuff it full, full, full. Then I hand-stitch the fourth side closed. Presto! Set your pillow on your couch, step back and admire your work: You are a designer! I like to clump three pillows together because they look great nestled next to each other.

These pillows make really nice gifts. Hang a cute tag on the pillow that says, "This pillow was created from one of my dearly loved Quacker sweaters. I filled it with good wishes just for you. Enjoy it because I've shared from my heart."

Another thing you can do is to cut the sleeves off of an old sweater. Then you take an old denim jacket that you've bought at a flea market or a thrift shop and start to play. The easiest way to make something quick is to cut the sleeves off the jacket and the sweater, making sure they are the same size. (This job requires a sewing machine, so I call on my daughter, Lee, for help. She has all the equipment and knows how to use it.) Once the sleeves are the right size, sew the knit sleeves on the denim jacket and vice versa. You now have two new outfits with your own special touch!

We can't all be Martha Stewart, but we can be our own special selves. While maybe some of us have a hard time thinking up a truly original idea, we all have some creativity in our center core. So, why not copy someone else's idea and make it your own? Let the Quacker Factory help you get started. Try things and be proud of everything you do. There is never a failure: The worst job in the whole world can always be fixed by adding some sparkle. Never, never give up.

Quack a Smile

Start where you are, use what you have, do what you can—it will be enough.

# Part Four

Wrap Up Some Good Cheer:
Giving from the Heart

# Finding the "Perfect" Gift

C hristmas is the most wonderful time of the year—especially if you're a professional planner. One day my friend Beth called to tell me, "I just bought my first Christmas present and it was for you." I was thrilled that the gift was for me, because, as you all know, it is all about us. But give me a break, Beth Ann, it was only a few months past the last Christmas! It was a bit early to be thinking about Christmas.

Shopping early for Christmas has always posed a problem for me. Where do you put the presents until Christmas so you don't forget you bought them? How do you keep from giving your gift to the person before Christmas? And how do you not overshop? It took me years of trial and error to figure it out.

I sold my house in Ripon in 1982 when my daughter Lee was eighteen years old and off to college. When I was packing up the house, I found four Barbie dolls, a Ken doll and enough teeny tiny clothes to last a lifetime. They had been shoved under the steps to the attic. I must have bought them when Lee was four or five years old and forgotten them. Even back then my mind may have been more cluttered than the attic stairs.

So I finally decided I would get all my Christmas decorations done early. If I started decorating before Thanksgiving and got everything up, then I could put all my effort into shopping. Well, that didn't work out well because the earlier I started decorating, the more places I found to decorate. Believe me, if you were around my house at that time of the year and were standing still for a few minutes, I would have decorated you! And, even so, I'd still be doing my Christmas shopping on Christmas Eve day. Not good. It made for very high stress levels. Between the guilt and the stress, I was starting to get sick of Christmas. Some years I'd feel guilty because my house wasn't decorated and my shopping wasn't done. Now, this whole "Christmas thing" was not rocket science or saving the starving in Biafra. I had to figure it out.

When my brother and I grew up, we got a check. So, when my kids got older, I thought, "Ah ha!" I found the solution to Christmas shopping: Just write a check and gift-wrap it. Well, my kids said "No!" They didn't care how small the gifts were; they wanted the fun and anticipation of presents under the tree. This was a challenge for me, because I always had trouble making up my mind what to give people. I always wanted it to be the perfect gift; the best anyone ever got in their life!

*Quack a Smile*

Wanted:
A jolly man bearing gifts!

Well, I just started buying stuff . . . lots of stuff. Everyone had to have equal amounts of stuff. Finally, one day, I sat and had a huge chat with me: "Jeanne, get a grip. You are killing the spirit of Christmas and you are killing your spirit." The solution? Ask for lists. My new motto has become: "No lists, no gifts!" This way, my crystal ball and psychic days are over. I give what people like, not what I think they would like. Problem solved.

And, if I can't find the right present on the list, I give gift certificates. I have become famous for my personalized gift certificates. I don't like store-bought gift cards because if you don't use them, you can lose them, or the store will take a percentage off.

So I give homemade gift certificates and I find really fun ways to present them. For instance, if a person asks for a fishing pole and I can't find the perfect one, I'll go to a thrift shop and find an old mounted fish. I'll put a hook in its mouth and attach the gift certificate: "Treat yourself to the best fishing pole. It's a treat from Santa. Happy Fishing!" Then I'll wrap it up very elaborately.

I have lots of fun finding really kitschy ways to do the certificates—I really have more fun giving them than I do giving the perfect gift!

These are the rules to my gift certificates:

**1** The recipient needs to present their gift selection to me with a bill for what they buy. If they don't have my original gift certificate, no payoff!

**2** They must use it within a year. You snooze . . . you lose!

**3** If they can't find what they asked for, then it falls through. No changing the gift to anything else, so they must choose their gift wisely.

**4** They must have fun collecting their gift. (I have fun giving, so please have fun receiving. Know that I have given it with love and joy! Receive it as such!)

**5** When I am dead and gone, they need to remember "Mom's Gift Certificates." I hope they keep the tradition alive.

So why not take the stress out of gift-giving? Wrap up a big 'ole stuffed fish this year and have yourself one big belly laugh over your silliness. Spread the joy!

# Homemade Candles to Melt Their Hearts

**E**very year my friends and I like to look around for a new holiday craft project. One November my friend said that she thought we could make candles a lot cheaper than buying them. All we had to do was melt down old candles and make new ones with the melted wax. The only additional cost would be to buy wicks and little metal tabs to hold them. So we started collecting old candles from our friends and family and ended up with boxes full of red, green and white candles.

Then we thought about what we could use to form the candles: milk cartons, half and half cartons, small whipping cream containers. (All of these work well because they hold hot wax, and, since they are wax-lined, you can just peel the outside away when the candle hardens and "voila!" you have a candle.)

Next we had to figure out how to melt the wax. We thought and thought about what we could do. This was when I lived in Wisconsin and our town of Ripon had an ice cream factory. In the '60s they used metal containers to store the ice cream. Wouldn't you know, these containers were exactly what we needed . . . and we found a way to appropriate some!

ere's what you do: First you have to break the candles up into small pieces so that they melt fast. Since wax can catch fire if it gets too hot, you want to make sure you keep your stove temperature on low! Put your chunks of wax in your melting container and slowly melt while stirring. Once the wax reaches a temperature of 190 degrees, turn off the heat and cover the pot. Let the wax sit for a while to get out all the bubbles.

While the wax is settling, prepare your container. Take one of the metal tabs and feed the wick through it. After you have determined the length of wick you'll need, tie the top of the wick to a pencil or a stick that is long enough to sit across the top of your container, making sure that the metal tab is flat on the bottom of the container. Make sure the wick is directly in the center of your container.

Pour the wax very slowly into the container and let it sit until it hardens. If you are really ambitious, you can melt several different colors of wax at the same time. Pour one layer first and let it cool. Pour a second layer of a different color next. Repeat until you have filled the container.

This is a fun way to while away a winter day! After your candles are all done, tie ribbons around them and bring them to holiday parties as hostess gifts. Your friends will appreciate how much time you spent making them yourself.

# Chocolate Spoons from Scratch

Looking for a perfect hostess gift or something for your coffee-loving coworkers? Whip up a batch of chocolate spoons, put a few in a bag and tie the bag to a pound of gourmet coffee.

To make a batch of 24:

24 heavy green and white plastic spoons
   (you can use silver spoons from your silverware
   drawer if you are keeping the spoons for yourself)
6 oz. white chocolate
6 oz. dark chocolate
Optional: Red and green sugars

Place waxed paper on two cookie sheets.
Put white and dark chocolate in two separate bowls. Melt each bowl of chocolate in the microwave. Dip the spoons in either of the chocolates and then set on the waxed paper with the handle of the spoon propped up on the side. Drizzle the spoon with the contrasting chocolate, then sprinkle the desired sugar color over the top. They look so pretty you almost hate to eat them (and I do mean . . . almost!)

Refrigerate the spoons until the chocolate is nice and hard. Wrap each spoon individually in cellophane and tie with a ribbon.

# Simmering Smells of the Season

There is nothing better than having people walk into your house and say, "Oh . . . it smells wonderful in here!"

Every year we make little potpourri bags for ourselves and plenty more to give out. It's a simple gesture that makes your house smell like home to all who enter.

For each bag you make, you'll need:

½ cup of dried or fresh orange peels

One 6-inch square of tulle fabric

2 crushed cinnamon sticks

8 drops of oil of orange

1 tablespoon whole cloves

1 piece of ribbon for tying fabric closed

In a bowl, mix orange peels, cloves and cinnamon. Add orange oil and mix. Place a large spoonful of the mixture onto the fabric and tie it up with ribbon. If you're giving them away, attach a little card to the ribbon that says: "Place the bag in two quarts of simmering water on the stove and enjoy!" It will make their home smell so good.

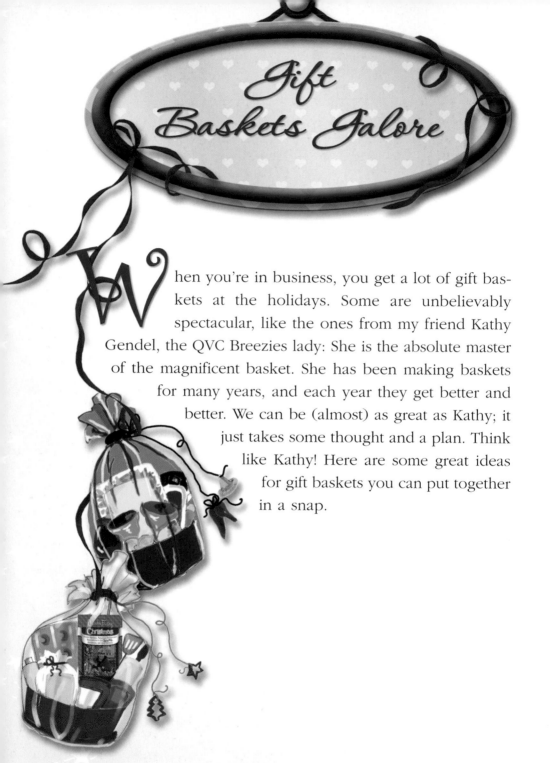

# Gift Baskets Galore

When you're in business, you get a lot of gift baskets at the holidays. Some are unbelievably spectacular, like the ones from my friend Kathy Gendel, the QVC Breezies lady: She is the absolute master of the magnificent basket. She has been making baskets for many years, and each year they get better and better. We can be (almost) as great as Kathy; it just takes some thought and a plan. Think like Kathy! Here are some great ideas for gift baskets you can put together in a snap.

# "Don't Put All Your Eggs in One Basket" Basket

- *Rooster salt & pepper shakers*
- *Recipes to make the perfect hard-boiled egg*
- *Deviled egg tray*
- *Jar of gourmet mustard*
- *Jar of capers*
- *Jar of mayonnaise*
- *Egg-shaped timer*
- *Egg slicer*
- *Recipe for great deviled eggs (I'm giving you a great one here to include. Make it an egg-stravaganza!)*

# Howard's Impish Deviled Eggs

## Makes 24 servings

**M**y assistant, Kate, tells a great story about these eggs:

"My dad was named 'Most Impish' when he was in high school, and that impishness continued throughout his colorful life. He would make these deviled eggs for parties and get-togethers. When I left home, I would call my dad for some of his recipes, and he never used measuring cups or measuring spoons. He would just say, 'Add some mayonnaise, some dry mustard, a little bit of Worcestershire and mix it all together, then taste it and add what you think is needed.'"

Hard-boil 12 eggs
Cut the eggs in half and scoop out the yolks into a small bowl

Mix in:

2/3 cup of mayonnaise
1/4 cup of finely chopped scallions
1 teaspoon Worcestershire sauce
1 teaspoon dry mustard
2 teaspoons ketchup
2 teaspoons celery seed
1 teaspoon onion powder
Pinch of salt
Pinch of pepper

Mix all ingredients together and then
scoop into a zip-top bag. Push the mixture all
the way down into one corner and then snip off the
corner with scissors. By squeezing the bag, you can
pipe the yolk mixture into the hole in the egg.

Sprinkle the eggs with paprika for a blast of color.

# "Fill Your Days
# with S'More Love" Basket

- Sterno
- Small terra cotta pot
- Package of bamboo skewers
- Homemade marshmallows
- Chocolate bars (Swiss)
- A great automatic lighter
- A pretty old tray to set them out on
- Box of graham crackers

164

## S'Mores

One day while I was on-air at QVC with Mary Beth Roe, she said she had just come back from Minnesota where she had attended a wedding. She stayed at a small old-fashioned motel on a lake that had the best tradition. Each room came equipped with Hershey Bars, a bag of marshmallows and a box of graham crackers. Every night they would have a huge bonfire down by the lake, and everyone would bring their supplies and gather together to make s'mores. Nobody knew anyone else at first, yet by the end of the night they were best of friends.

I thought, "Boy, what a great idea." So I came home and bought all the supplies and a fire pit for the pool area. Well, as good ideas go, I never did do it with company. It was just too much effort getting the fire pit set up and working. Building a fire is man's work!

But in my head I loved the idea. Then one winter we went to dinner with David Fritz, our cruise director, in Fort Myers, Florida. We went to a great restaurant, and I noticed that an interesting dessert was arriving at nearby tables and people were giggling. We asked the waitress what it was and she said, "They're making s'mores." Well, they were having the time of their lives, and suddenly I had the solution to my "sticky" dilemma—no pun intended.

I could definitely handle the way they were making them at the table. Basically, here's what you do: Get out a big tray (I like to use a silver one). You can add a step by making "formal s'mores." It's also a great fire and mess protector.

You gather one small terra cotta pot for each guest and place it on the tray with a small can of Sterno in each pot. Put marshmallows, chocolate bars and graham crackers all around the tray with some bamboo skewers (Let the skewers soak in water for a while first so they won't burn so fast).

When you're ready to make your s'mores, put a marshmallow on the stick and roast it over the Sterno. (Be very careful when doing this.) Take your time roasting it so the marshmallow gets really squishy in the center and golden on the outside. While your right hand is roasting, your left hand can set up your graham cracker. Put a piece of chocolate on it and have the other cracker ready to top it all off. When the marshmallow is perfect, put it on top of the chocolate bar and top with the other cracker. Smush it down good so that is oozy and perfect. Rejoice in every calorie. It's worth it.

# "Life Is One Big Memory" Basket

- Scrapbook supplies, like a scrapbook and pretty paper
- A couple of packages of cute scrapbook accessories
- A pair of pretty scissors
- A couple of glue sticks
- A couple of disposable cameras
- A couple of great scrapbooking magazines

Put together some of your favorite scrapbook ideas for them to use. Add pictures of the friend you are giving the basket to on some of the pages. . . . She will know that she is very much loved!

# Life's Just Ducky Basket

- A rubber ducky
- Yellow bath salts
- Candles
- Bars of duck soap
- A singing duck . . . "You Are My Sunshine"
- A big, big fluffy bath sheet
- Ducky slippers
- Ducky robe
- Bubbles to blow
- A "feel-good" book
- A copy of The Quacker Factory's "Lucky Ducky Stress Relief" story on the next page
- Write a cute ducky love note

## Lucky Ducky Stress Relief

The top-notch researchers who staff our high-tech lab at The Quacker Factory are involved in much more than the development of exciting new apparel for our loyal Quacker fans. We have a whole team devoted to putting more joy into life and getting all the stress out of it. These scientists have chosen, as a model for this project, the common duck.

The duck, as many of us know, has a distinct trait that we humans would do well to emulate. They move along the surface of the lake in a graceful and completely unruffled fashion while, under the surface of the water, they are indeed paddling like hell. Our research has shown that it is important to reach this stress-free state where everything you need to get done seems to happen by itself.

As a means to this end, our "Quack" scientists have developed a kit that will help to eliminate the stress from our lives so we can more effectively enjoy ourselves in all our pursuits. Use of the basket is quite simple. First, light the candles and put on some soft, relaxing music. Start a hot tub and prop your sunshine singin' duck up on the tub edge right by you. Lucky duckies have a fine dust under their wings. You have been supplied with a portion of this elixir. Put it in your bath and it bubbles up and brings joy to all who submerge. Float your rubber duck in this warm and lathery tub. Bring along your ducky soap. Make sure before you hop in the tub that your towel, robe and slippers are all handy for when you emerge a much more relaxed duckling!

This will definitely put you in a "Quacky" state of mind as you linger in a relaxing bubble bath surrounded by images of our friend, the duck, from whom we've learned so much. Blow some bubbles and watch them float in the air . . . let your imagination float with them! Oh, life really is just ducky!

## "Life Is a Bowl of Cherries" Basket

- *Erma Bombeck book,* If Life Is a Bowl of Cherries, What Am I Doing in the Pits?

- *Cherry-scented candles*

- *A cute coffee mug with cherries on it*

- *Can of cherry pie filling*

- *A cute recipe card with "Life Is a Bowl of Cherries" recipe on it*

- *A pretty pie plate or four great parfait glasses*

# Life Is a Bowl of Cherries

## Makes 4 parfait glasses

L ife is a bowl of cherries . . . pits and all! In this case, life is a parfait glass of cherries!

1 package cream cheese softened (8 oz.)
½ cup sugar
2 cups Cool Whip
1 can cherry pie filling, divided (20 oz.)

Mix cream cheese and sugar in a bowl until smooth and gently stir in Cool Whip.

In parfait glasses, layer ¼ cup cream cheese mixture and 2 tablespoons cherry pie filling. Repeat layers until you reach the top of the glass. This makes enough for four parfait glasses.

If cherry isn't your favorite flavor, you can always substitute any other flavor of pie filling. No matter what you use, this is decadent!

# "If God Gives You Lemons Make Margaritas" Basket

*A package of Crystal Lite on-the-go packets*

*A bottle of margarita mix*

*A bottle of tequila*

*2 cute margarita glasses*

*A container of margarita salt*

*A bag of tortilla chips*

*A jar of great salsa*

*A bottle of aspirin for the morning after*

*A great recipe for a salsa cheese dip . . . I just happen to have one you are going to love, love, love!*

174

# Cheesy Picante

16 oz. Velveeta cheese—cubed
1 jar picante sauce (6 oz.) mild or hot

This is so easy . . .just put the cubes of Velveeta in a microwave-safe bowl. Pour the picante over the top and microwave slowly, stirring often so that it doesn't burn. Serve hot out of the microwave on Frito's Scoops!

quacky
Tip

Want daiquiris in a hurry? Make a big batch of your favorite daiquiri. Put plastic Ziplock bags into the daiquiri glasses and fill bags with the mixture. Zip 'em up and pop them into the freezer. Great to have for a party or a personal emergency!

# "Proud to Be an American" Basket

- Little yard flags for patriotic holidays

- A couple boxes of sparklers

- A pretty red, white and blue hat to go with their Quacker Americana clothing

- A kazoo for them to hum their favorite patriotic tunes

- An apple pie you baked from scratch—I always include the recipe also

- A baseball autographed by the local baseball team

176

# Sour Cream Apple Pie
## Makes 8 servings

4 cups apples, peeled
and sliced

½ pint sour cream (I prefer
Breakstone but not the
light or fat-free!)

4 tablespoons flour

¾ cup sugar

1 teaspoon cinnamon

½ cup brown sugar

One 9-inch pie shell, unbaked

Topping:

¼ cup butter

1 teaspoon cinnamon

⅓ cup sugar

⅓ cup flour

Combine apples, sour cream, flour, sugar, cinnamon and brown sugar in a bowl and mix well. Pour into pie shell. Combine all topping ingredients and sprinkle over apple filling. Bake at 425 degrees for about 15 minutes. Leave the pie in the oven and turn down the heat to 350 degrees. Bake for another 50 minutes.

quacky Tip

Well, I'm not really one to spend all day in the kitchen baking a pie . . . but this one is easy and well worth the effort! Besides, you can get presliced and peeled apples in a bag in your produce department, which really makes it easy.

Wrap your baskets up with cellophane and lots of ribbon. Add a little dangle to your basket like a rubber ducky on the Life's Just Ducky basket, or a flag pin on the Proud to Be an American basket. Let your imagination run wild.

Oh my gosh, you *are* just as great as Kathy. Life is a "Breezie!"

# Part Five

Family Favorites:
Memories & Meals that
Nourish Our Hearts & Souls

# Food of the
# Angels

One of my favorite childhood memories was Mom's snow ice cream. In Wisconsin, we had lots of blizzards. I don't remember ever getting snow days. Even if it snowed hard overnight, you just got up and walked to school in the middle of the road.

I remember once after a storm a neighbor stopped by and asked my dad, who was outside shoveling, if I would like a ride with his family to school. My dad shouted back to him that I would have better memories if I walked, since it was such a beautiful day. Beautiful? Well, there was probably ten feet of snow and it was at least five degrees below zero, but my dad thought I could use the exercise. God love him, he really believed that. You know, he walked five miles to school and back, while I only walked eight blocks.

During Christmas vacation, if we had a really pretty snowstorm, my mom would say, "Let's have a party. Go outside and bring me in big bowls of fresh snow." But she would always caution us: "Make sure you only get the fresh snow and not any with yellow stains!" When we brought in the snow, she would pour

Carnation Sweetened Condensed Milk over it with some sugar and a sprinkling of her good vanilla. She'd stir it up and give it to my brother and me to eat quickly so it didn't melt. We thought it was the food of the angels!

On a snowy day, give everyone a spoon, sit on the front porch and munch away. It's a memory-maker.

## Snow Ice Cream

### Makes 6 servings

12-oz. can of evaporated milk
1½ teaspoons vanilla extract
¾ cup white sugar
1 gallon fresh snow

In a large, chilled bowl, combine evaporated milk, vanilla and sugar until smooth. Gradually stir in snow until the mixture reaches the consistency you like.

Dish out into chilled bowls and eat right away!

# Santa Wally

## By Lee Bice

During our three-week Bice Christmas extravaganza in Fort Lauderdale, we would stay at a little family-run motel. It was the kind of place people would return to year after year, so we usually knew almost everyone who stayed there. Every year on Christmas Eve, the hotel owners would put together a spread and break out some champagne for any of the guests who wanted to partake. They did this early in the evening so it didn't intrude on anybody's plans for the night, and, boy, did we have plans. Christmas Eve we went to visit my grandparents' friends, Claude and Lee. Claude and Lee were also from Wisconsin but wintered in Florida. There were several other couples, all my grandparents' age, who were also invited. My brother, Tim, and I were the only kids. Needless to say, the first year we went, we were less than thrilled. "What? Get out of the pool to spend a night with old people?" Of course, Mom had little sympathy for this attitude and off we went.

When we arrived, there were hugs and kisses from everyone and much cheek-pinching and *My how you've growns.* Then Tim and I would go out to the back by the pool and stick our feet in the water. It wouldn't be long before Mom would come out and make us get our butts back inside.

One of the couples who would join us every year was

Wally and Essie. Essie was *Santa Wally* the biggest culprit when it came to cheek-pinching; Wally generally settled for a handshake. He was a big, round man who didn't like to stand if he didn't have to. Once all the adults were there and settled down with their highballs, Lee would bustle about putting together the buffet. Ham sandwiches, mounds of deviled eggs and cheesecake from Wolfies, the best bakery in town. After dinner it was more highballs for the adults.

And time for carols. We'd all gather around, and with my dad playing organ, we'd belt 'em out. Usually around this time, Wally would sneak away unnoticed. After the singing was done, there would be a knock on the door. "Who could that be at this time of night?" Wink, wink. Lee would answer the door. "Look, it's Santa!"

"Ho, ho, ho! Are there any good boys or girls here tonight?" My brother and I would yell, "Yes!" And in walked Santa. I wasn't fooled. I knew better. That wasn't Santa; it was Santa Wally. He'd come in, take a seat, and pull a few presents out of his sack for us. Then he'd sit back, pick up his highball and tell off-color stories the rest of the night.

I'll always hold a special place in my heart for Santa Wally. What a kind man to have bought a Santa suit, stored it year after year, for the enjoyment of two kids he saw once a year. Now THAT is the true spirit of the holiday.

# Jingle Bells and Puppies

## By Lee Bice

All my life, I've wanted a dog. I prayed for one. I begged for one. I wrote to Santa every Christmas asking him to bring me one. No dice. Turns out I'm allergic to dogs. Even after going to friends' houses who had dogs and coming home with swollen eyes and hives, I still wanted one. My mother's mantra was, "Don't touch the dog, Lee," because inevitably I would be drawn to any dog I saw. Then I grew up, well, older at any rate, and outgrew most of my allergies. I got married, and my husband and I finally bought a home of our own. Now it was my time for a dog. So off Mike and I went to the Humane Society—no pure-bred dog for us. We wanted to save a mutt. And there we found Sasha, a beautiful one-year-old Rhodesian ridge-back mix with short hair (I said I grew out of most of my allergies). I fell in love instantly, before we even got her home.

When we did get her home, we found out why she had been at the shelter. Never having had a dog before, it didn't occur to me I needed to have stuff in the house for a dog *before* I brought the dog home.

So into the bathroom she went, and off to the pet shop we went. We got home loaded with doggie gear and went to greet our new baby in the bathroom—only the bathroom was gone, replaced with a large pile of rubble on top of which stood Sasha. Off to the phone book to find a trainer. The trainer said she had separation anxiety, and after she pulled off an incredible Harry Houdini escape, he brought us the true and undisputed love of our lives: Osa, a rottweiler.

Shortly before Christmas, Mike and I were shopping for a present for our new puppy, Osa, when we found a jingle bell collar. It was candy red nylon with six large jingle bells bolted around the collar. We thought it the best thing ever and bought it right away. This was before everyone got on the frilly dress-up-your-dog train, so decorating your dog was a new concept for us. We were charmed. But we were nothing compared to how charmed our Osa was. She loved that thing from the first time she heard it. She couldn't wait to get it on, and when she did, she hopped around to make it ring; she'd shake her head and roll around on the ground, just so she could listen to the collar tinkle. After the holidays were over, I took the collar off to put it away until the next year. Osa was distraught. She sniffed around the house for days looking for it. Eventually she got

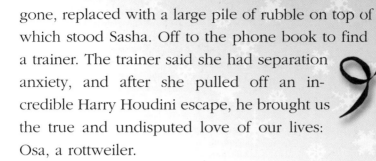

over it and life resumed as normal. When the next year rolled around and I pulled that collar out and gave it a jingle, Osa came bounding in from the other room, practically knocking me down in her haste to get to it. She pushed her head up under my hands, stuck her nose through the loop and urged me to hurry up and put it on her. Every year she would wear it with such happiness and pride you couldn't help but be joyful when you were with her.

When I got my next dog, Winslow the dachshund, I immediately got him a smaller green version of the same collar. When he saw how much Osa loved hers, nothing would do but to have his put on right away. He loves his just as much. In fact, after Osa died, Winslow was handling it fine until the day I decided to get rid of Osa's things. When he heard the bells, he headed into a depression that *forced* me to get two new puppies. Now he's happy again, and this year we're off to the store for new jingle bell collars for Gabby and Dolly.

## Quack a Smile

Remember,
everytime you hear a bell ring,
an angel gets her wings.

# The Sure Shot Shooting Gallery

## By Tim Bice

When I was seven years old, the Sure Shot Shooting Gallery was it: The holy grail of all possible Christmas gifts; The Tickle Me Elmo for the ages; the absolute must-have, daydream toy for every boy and most of the girls in my then very young life.

Old west movies were the entertainment of choice. Cowboys and Indians was the number-one game played in our neighborhood. And, there was nothing that could turn you into a genuine sharp shooter faster than a Sure Shot Shooting Gallery.

I don't remember now whether or not the cheap plastic gun actually shot anything at the cheap plastic tin cans or if it actually worked at all. I do know that it was nowhere near as slick as today's PlayStation II, where kids can point a real-looking gun at a real-looking cowboy and shoot him dead with gore and all. And I know we can't go back and review the Bice family super-8 home movies and see young Tim playing with the grand-daddy of all Christmas gifts. Why? Because I never got one.

Yes, it's true. Every year, for what was easily a third of my young life (maybe two years?), the Sure Shot Shooting Gallery was the one and only item on my Christmas list. I sent this list to the North Pole. I sat on every Santa's lap and begged the bearded chaps for one. And, of course, I whined and whined all year long to my poor parents. Alas, it was not meant to be.

Then, one year when we were on our family Christmas trip to Florida, something happened. A few days before Christmas we were at the hotel getting ready to go to Grandma and Grandpa's for dinner. We all went out to the car to toss in some sweaters and other things to keep Lee and I busy. All four of us were behind the car, and when Dad popped the lid, we were greeted by the most incredible golden glow and a chorus of heavenly angels. There, nestled in the trunk of that lowly rent-a-car, was the Holy Grail! You guessed it! The Sure Shot Shooting Gallery.

*Bam!!* The trunk lid was slammed. We kids were hustled into the backseat and rode in silence to our grandparents' house while an ice storm raged in South Florida between Mom and Dad in the front seat of that rental car. There was never another word spoken in front of us kids about "The Incident."

I couldn't wait for Christmas morning, because I knew for sure that gun-shooting glory was soon to be mine. The day finally arrived with our living room resembling a showroom floor at FAO Schwartz. As the wrapping paper lay scattered

*Tim, the buckaroo*

around the room and all of the gifts were opened and accounted for, lo and behold, there was neither a gun nor a gallery to be seen.

I would show no sign of disappointment. This would be a point of pride. This day was somehow a rite of passage: The year the great Santa Claus question became a moot point. This day, young Tim was ready to become . . . a big kid.

So how did that Sure Shot Shooting Gallery end up in the trunk of the car, and where had it gone? Was the whole incident a figment of my imagination?

Later in life I came to find out my parents weren't just being mean in denying my repeated requests. Every year they tried to get the toy, but it was so popular they could never find one. That fateful year Dad stumbled across one by accident and had the great misfortune to forget he had placed it in the trunk. (My parents had a long-standing rule that if a present was seen before Christmas you wouldn't get it.) And, in what was a roller-coaster of emotions for my parents, they decided that since the surprise was gone, it just wasn't meant to be. They took the toy to a local church's toy drive where it made some young kid very happy. And, I learned for "shooting-sure" that Christmas isn't really about what we get, but about what we have and what we give back.

# Counting Santas

## By Lee Bice

I don't remember how it started, but I count Santas. I imagine it was probably a suggestion from my mom. You see, when staying in Florida every Christmas holiday, we'd usually go out somewhere for dinner. Of course, this seriously interrupted me and Tim's pool time. Like most kids, we lived in the pool the whole time we were there. Then Mom would say the dreaded words. "Oh, Butch, let's take a ride." Groan. It was bad enough I had to get out of the pool for dinner, but to go driving slowly down every little road looking at million-dollar homes just wasn't my bag. I'm sure I was vocal about that, and that was probably when Mom made her suggestion. I'm betting it was something along the lines of:

"Why don't you just find something to do to keep yourself occupied?"

"Like what?"

"I don't know, count Santas or something!"

By this Mom meant the Santa decorations that people had put in their yards and on their houses. So I did. I don't remember how many I counted that first time, but I do know that last year I got well over two hundred. Yep, I still do it every year. Over time it has become a growing ritual. Each year I make up new rules to make sure there is no cheating or getting carried away. People started asking me: "How many did you get this year, Lee?" It has become such a part of being me that I think if I decided not to do it one year my family and friends would have me hospitalized for fear I was ill.

So now not only do I actually *enjoy* driving around after dinner, Mom goes out of her way to make sure I get all over the city to get as many Santas for my count as I can. She chafes at my rules—she is a natural-born cheater—but I tell her, "Hey, if you don't like it, count your own snowmen."

## BoWs, BoWs, BoWs

I guess you could say I'm quirky. Always have been. Since I was little, whenever I received a present, if it had a bow on it, I'd pull it off and put it on my head. You could tell if I had a truly bountiful Christmas because my head would look like one of those paper-plate wedding bouquets they make for the bride at her shower. Wearing bows puts a smile on everyone's face and makes you feel good. And, yes, I still do it now—especially in restaurants. Give it a try sometime. There's nothing better than laughter.

—Lee Bice

*Lee and Tim*

# Get in the Spirit and Hold On Tight

Both of my kids went to college in New York City, so I took to going to the Big Apple for Thanksgiving. It became our tradition to kick off the Christmas season at 2:00 A.M. the night before Thanksgiving. We'd go down to where they were setting up the floats for the Macy's Day parade. We'd watch as they blew up the huge balloons; it made us feel like we were really a part of the parade.

Then, as dawn neared, we would walk back to our hotel and fall asleep. The next day, we didn't have to watch the parade on TV because we'd been a part of putting it together. When we got up late on Thanksgiving, we would wander back out into the city, have Thanksgiving dinner with the hot dog vendor on the street corner, and then wander through the city looking at all the beautiful Christmas windows—they were magical. And, even though our fun was almost free, we felt like we were living large in New York City.

When my kids got married, we took their spouses, Karin and Mike, to New York to share our traditions with them. They grew to love it as much as we did.

This year, Lee and I took Lori, who works at Quacker Factory, and her daughter, Kyla, to share our

Christmas Macy's Day parade tradition with them. Late at night we walked around and watched the activity of putting the Macy's Thanksgiving Day parade together once more. We looked for new balloons and new floats, but mostly I watched the faces of all the children. It was a wonderful evening. Then, the next day we started a new tradition: We had Thanksgiving dinner at the Tavern on the Green in Central Park. Oh, this was more magical than the parade. Imagine thousands and thousands of tiny white lights sparkling off crystal chandeliers. We could just feel the Christmas spirit.

Try to capture this spirit at the *beginning* of the season each year, then hold onto it in your heart. This way, there's much less room for stress and feeling frazzled. Christmas is too wonderful to let it get ugly. Celebrate with your friends; make it merry and bright. Be a kid again, just for the season.

I Love New York

# Great Memories

Me and my friends

My dad and brother
Christmas in Florida

My family
at
Christmas

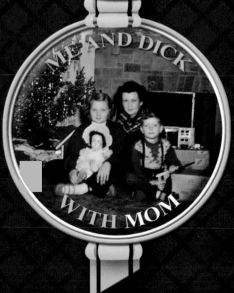

ME AND DICK WITH DAD

ME AND DICK WITH MOM

*My Grandma and Grandpa Freund*

My favorite Uncle Jack, Aunt Madeline, my mom, Dick and me

# Family

My kids Tim and Lee

Even at an early age I taught my kids to really fill up a tree!

ME ORCHESTRATING CHRISTMAS

My brother Dick and his kids, Margaret and Rickie

Love Remember Celebrate Cherish Celebrate Love Remember Celebrate

Celebrate

Remember

*Love*

Family is very important to me. After my husband died, we had the test as a family to either fall apart or grow closer and make "Butchie" really proud of us. We're a very close-knit family; in fact, we run The Quacker Factory together. My children are a huge part of my life. They make me giggle, and I hope they make you giggle, too.

Lee and Tim

Tim, Lee, my mom Mora and my niece Margaret

197

# The Perfect Tree

Dick and his wife Nancy

Dick's Perfect Tree

My brother, Dick, has the perfect tree here, but come on, Dickie, fill it up with more ornaments! Don't be stingy!

But, for two kids whose Christmas was run by a "bah-humbug" mom, I think we got the idea of what a perfect tree is. I think it's great we both love Christmas so much. Merry Christmas, little brother! May all your holiday wishes come true!

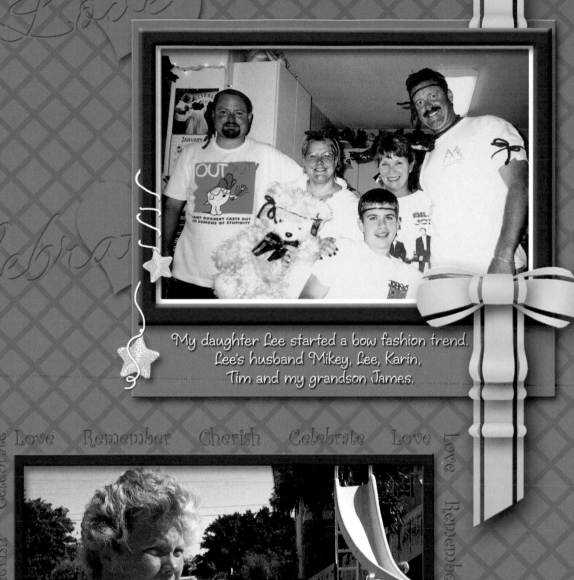

My daughter Lee started a bow fashion trend.
Lee's husband Mikey, Lee, Karin,
Tim and my grandson James.

Love    Remember    Cherish    Celebrate    Love

Me in
Florida at
Christmas

# More All-Time Favorite Recipes

This book is full of recipes for special occasions. Over the years, friends and family have shared many of these recipes with me. Other recipes I learned to create at the side of Madame Kuony at the Postillion in Fond du Lac, Wisconsin. All of them are offered to you in the hope that they will bring you and your loved ones joy and treasured memories. We hope these recipes will become some of your favorites.

Most people don't allow themselves to splurge like this every day, so when they do, they are looking for something totally sinful and full of intense flavor. Most of these recipes can be made low fat by using a little common sense, but remember, there are many calories in this world that don't count at all.

These are the times when calories don't count:

- Holidays and birthdays.

- Fanny Mae candy sent with love from a friend.

- A bite of your kids' food . . . those calories belong to the kids.

- A shared dessert! These go to the person who ordered.

- Tasting: This is an act of kindness so as not to hurt the host's feelings.

- Tasting while cooking: This is for the betterment of the family meal.

- Eating in the grocery store, but only if you eat the item before you pay and save the packaging to pay at the checkout. (Remember, if you don't pay, you double your calories!)

- Food that doesn't taste as good as it looks.

- Anything consumed while on a cruise.

Quack a Smile

Too much of a good thing
is wonderful.

# French Toast Bake

## Makes 10 servings

id I mention how much I loved the flavor of pralines? This is an awesome breakfast dish that will leave your family shouting for more.

8 eggs
1½ cups half and half
⅓ cup maple syrup
⅓ cup light brown sugar, packed
10 to 12 slices of bread, 1-inch thick

Topping:

½ cup butter
⅔ cup maple syrup

½ cup light brown sugar, packed
2 cups chopped pecans

Generously butter a 13 x 9-inch casserole dish. Mix eggs, half and half, maple syrup and sugar in a bowl. Place bread slices in the casserole dish and cover with egg mixture. Cover with plastic wrap and soak overnight in the refrigerator.

Preheat oven to 350 degrees and remove casserole from refrigerator. Make the topping next. Melt butter in a saucepan. Add sugar and maple syrup and cook for 1 or 2 minutes. Stir in pecans. Pour this mixture over the bread and bake for 45 to 55 minutes. Let it sit for 10 minutes before serving.

**quacky Tip**

You don't have to be stuck with plain old white bread . . . Sometimes I even use cinnamon raisin bread. There are many different breads to choose from, so pick your favorite.

# Lee & Mike's "Special Friends" Egg Squares

My son-in-law Mike always shared a special breakfast with my daughter, Lee. Neither of them wanted anything fancy. . . . They just enjoyed spending the time together. Mike was a handy guy in the kitchen and Lee just loved being cooked for!

For each serving:
2 eggs (whipped)
3 slices bread (½-inch cubed—better stale!)
1 stick butter

Melt butter. Add bread and cook until butter is absorbed and cubes are browned well. Cover with eggs and stir and cook until well done.

Optional—may be topped with sliced or shredded cheese.

# Bacon Cherry Poppers

These are so good. I actually will take the mixture and put it on a "quacker" too. It's great on anything! I'll also make it a bit easier and use the precooked bacon . . . it really saves time.

1 pound bacon, fried and crumbled
    (or you can use precooked)
¼ cup finely chopped green onion
2 tablespoons parsley
2 tablespoons Parmesan cheese
    (best if you use the real stuff)
½ cup Miracle Whip
24 cherry tomatoes

Combine all ingredients except tomatoes, in a bowl. Slice off the very top of the cherry tomatoes and scoop out the centers with a melon scoop or a tiny spoon. Fill the tomatoes with the mixture and refrigerate at least 2 hours before serving. The longer they sit before serving, the better they taste! Makes 2 dozen.

If you do put it on "quackers," you need to chop off the bottom of the cherry tomato or use regular tomatoes like a BLT. Nick, the food stylist who brings us food on our QVC shows, cuts out pretty bread rounds, toasts them and puts the mixture on the top.

# Baked Brie in Puff Pastry

This is such an elegant appetizer and it's so easy! You can make this up the day before and just heat it before you serve it. Rice crackers or some big-scoop Fritos are great with this.

1 sheet of frozen puff pastry, thawed
   (I like Pepperidge Farm)
1 wheel (8 oz.) of brie cheese
¼ cup sliced almonds
1 egg white, beaten

Preheat oven to 350 degrees. Lightly grease a 9-inch pie pan. Cut the brie in half so that you have 2 thin rounds. Place the pastry dough on the bottom of the pie pan so it lays over the edges. Place the first round of Brie on the pastry. Sprinkle the almonds on top of the first wheel of brie and cover with the other half. Bring the pastry dough up around the brie and make sure that it's all covered. Seal the edges of the pastry with a little water on your fingers.

Take a pastry brush and brush the pastry with the beaten egg white. This makes it look so pretty after it's baked. Bake in the oven at 350 degrees for 15 to 20 minutes until pastry is lightly browned. Let it sit for 5 minutes before serving.

quacky

Tip

There are a number of great
things you can fill the center
of the brie with. Sometimes I'll use
berries or different kids of nuts.
Another great way to serve
this is filled with a mixture of
sautéed mushrooms and onions,
drained well.

207

# Barbecue Shrimp Bites

## Makes 12–24 shrimp bites

As appetizers go, this one never lasts long enough to cool down! When you make these for a cocktail party, you can smell them as they are baking and mouths will water long before they come out of the oven.

1 pound of peeled, deveined shrimp, raw
(I use the big ones)
2 pounds of sliced bacon
1 bottle of barbecue sauce
Toothpicks

Preheat oven to 375 degrees. Wash the shrimp really well in a strainer and allow the water to drain. Take them out of the strainer and dry well.

Wrap a slice of bacon around each shrimp, covering it completely; then lay it down on a cookie sheet lined with aluminum foil with the end of the bacon facing down.

With a pastry brush, lightly brush the shrimp bites with barbecue sauce. Bake for about 15 minutes, checking all the while, until the outside of the bacon is crisp. This will ensure that the shrimp is completely cooked. When they are done, brush them with a bit more barbecue sauce and put back in the oven for 2 minutes so the barbecue sauce gets gooey.

Remove from oven and insert toothpicks into each one. Remove from the cookie sheet and place on a nice platter to serve warm.

# Christmas Tree Bread

## Makes 10–12 servings

Be warned: This bread takes a bit longer to put together, but it's worth it.

3 cups milk
½ cup granulated sugar
1 large egg, yolk and white separated
¾ cup diced dried fruit mix
2 ½ cups all-purpose flour
1 tablespoon baking powder
1 ½ teaspoons pumpkin pie spice (or ¾ tsp.
    ground cinnamon and ¾ tsp. ground cloves)
½ teaspoon salt
1 stick cold, unsalted butter, cut into small pieces
Granulated sugar

Make sure one rack is in the bottom third of oven and heat oven to 425 degrees. Measure milk in a 2-cup measuring cup, add sugar and egg yolk; stir to mix well. Stir in dried fruit. Let stand until you are ready to use.

Put flour, baking powder, spice and salt into large bowl and mix well. Add butter and cut in with pastry knife or with fingers, until mixture looks like fine granules. Stir milk mixture and pour over flour mixture. Stir with a fork until a soft dough forms. Turn out dough onto lightly floured surface and give 10 kneads. (If very sticky, let stand 3 or 4 minutes or add a little more flour.) Cut off about ¼ of dough.

Put remaining dough on an ungreased cookie sheet at least 16 inches long. Using both a rolling pin and fingers, pat and roll dough into a flat triangle about 12 inches long and 9 inches wide across the bottom. With scissors, make about ten diagonal cuts down each long side of the triangle, cutting to within about 1 inch of the center. Shape a small piece of reserved dough into a trunk at bottom of tree and remaining dough into a "pot." Dough may now be covered with plastic wrap and refrigerated for a couple hours or frozen for up to 2 weeks.

Bake tree 10 minutes. Beat egg white with a fork until broken up. Brush over hot bread, sprinkle with sugar. Bake 5 to 8 minutes longer, until light brown. With two spatulas, carefully transfer tree to a wire rack. If possible, cool at least 2 hours before serving. Let guests break off small pieces.

211

# Cocktail Sausages and Jelly

I know this sounds a bit strange, but it is a favorite among my party guests and it is so easy.

¾ cup grape jelly
¾ cup Dijon mustard
2 pounds cocktail sausages
(I like the little Oscar Mayer ones)

Mix jelly and mustard in a small slow cooker and add the sausages. Turn the slow cooker on high and simmer for 2 hours until the sausages are heated through. Put a small container of toothpicks next to the slow cooker to serve. You can also put these ingredients in a saucepan and heat more quickly if need be.

# Dilly Dip

**W**hen we had our retail shop, we sold a product called Dip-Idy-Dill. This was the best to serve on anything, and we always had a bowl of it sitting out in the shop. If you can't find this product, you can always make your own:

1 cup of Hellmann's mayonnaise (It must be Hellmann's or it will never taste right)
1 cup sour cream
$\frac{1}{2}$ cup finely chopped onions
1 tablespoon dill weed
$\frac{1}{2}$ teaspoon dry parsley

Mix all ingredients together until smooth. Let sit for half an hour in the refrigerator, and it is perfection!

# Kate's Famous Ham Rolls

## Makes about 40

My assistant, Kate, is a great cook. She is always bringing new and wonderful recipes into my world. This one is so easy, but it's always one of the first to go! Don't plan for leftovers.

1 package (8 oz.) of cream cheese, softened
1 small jar of green olives, chopped fine
1 small can of black olives, chopped fine
1 small jar of pimientos, chopped fine
1 pound of thickly sliced boiled ham from
    the deli
Toothpicks

In a medium bowl, mix the softened cream cheese with the green and black olives and pimiento until all the olives are covered well and the cream cheese is really soft.

Lay out a piece of ham and spread the mixture on it evenly . . . just a light coating of it, but not so light that you can see through it. Roll the piece of ham jelly-roll style and place it on a plate. Repeat this procedure with the rest of the ham.

Cover the plate and place in the refrigerator until ready to serve. Right before serving, bring the plate out and cut the pieces of ham into ¾ inch bites. Put a toothpick through each bite and put them on a great platter to serve. Easy and very, very good!

# Mini Sausage Wraps

3 packages of mini smoked sausages (10 oz.)
2 pounds bacon, cut in half
1 cup brown sugar
Toothpicks

Wrap each sausage with a bacon piece and secure with a toothpick. Put them on a nonstick cookie sheet and sprinkle generously with the brown sugar. Bake at 350 degrees until the bacon is done, about 45 minutes to an hour. Serve warm.

# Pesto Christmas Tree Treats

## Makes about 12 servings

This is so easy and so cute. It's one of the most irresistible appetizers I make, and everyone tells me how adorable they are!

1 package (8 oz.) cream cheese
⅓ cup premade pesto (pick your favorite)
Cinnamon stick
Red pepper, chopped fine

Cut the cream cheese in half diagonally. Place triangles together to form a Christmas tree shape on a serving plate (I use a Christmas tree plate). Top with the pesto and insert a cinnamon stick at the base of the triangle for the "tree trunk." Use chopped red pepper to decorate the "tree" . . . make the red pepper look like the ornaments.

Serve with your favorite crackers.

# Spinach Mushroom Caps

## Makes 25 to 30 caps

If you use fresh grated Parmesan cheese in this recipe it makes it so much better than cheese out of a can!

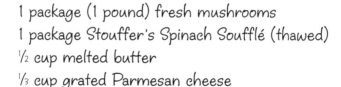

1 package (1 pound) fresh mushrooms
1 package Stouffer's Spinach Soufflé (thawed)
½ cup melted butter
⅓ cup grated Parmesan cheese

Preheat oven to 350 degrees. Pull stems off of mushrooms, reserving the mushroom caps. Chop the stems up really tiny. Mix the stems into the spinach and stir well. Dip the mushroom caps into the melted butter and arrange on a baking sheet. Fill the caps with the spinach mixture and sprinkle generously with Parmesan cheese. Bake for 15 to 20 minutes until the mushrooms get puffy and lightly browned. Serve warm.

If the mushroom caps are extra large, I fry them in butter 'til they are slightly soft. I think it adds more flavor to the finished dish.

# Wisconsin Beer Biscuits

## Makes about 16 biscuits

Wisconsin is known for a lot of things, but among the most recognizable are beer and cheese. These beer biscuits are the best!

4 cups Bisquick
⅓ to ½ cup sugar (depending on
   how sweet you want them)
One can of your favorite beer (12 oz.)
2 tablespoons melted butter
Shredded cheddar cheese (optional)

Preheat oven to 400 degrees. Mix all ingredients except cheese in a bowl. Pour into greased muffin tins. Bake for 15 to 20 minutes. If you are using cheese, sprinkle lightly on top of the biscuits about 5 minutes before they are done baking. Serve with a flavored butter (honey butter is the best!).

Sugar

# Who Made the Salad?

When I was a child, my mom's idea of a salad was half a canned pear or peach on a salad plate with a piece of lettuce underneath it. For company, she would take a canned pear half and soak it in her special sauce. She made that by cooking red hots candy in water until the candy melted. Then she set the pears in this until it cooled. She took the pears out and chilled them. Now she had cinnamon pears. She'd put them on salad plates with one skimpy piece of Bibb lettuce. In the center of the pear, she would put a little ball of cream cheese mixed with pecans. She'd put a few candy sprinkles over it for garnish. Sometimes she'd get really gourmet and add a clump of sugared grapes. God love her, I used this salad for years when I entertained. I thought I was Julia Child!

Now, I don't know if she did this because it was hard to get lettuce in the forties and fifties. That very well may have been the reason, but if it was, I'm not sure why it never changed when lettuce was very abundant again! In the spring, Mom serves garden lettuce. It was leafy lettuce with milk and sugar over it. Yummy! She'd serve this over new boiled potatoes, which might explain my size . . .

Have fun with the fifties salads during the holidays. They

are so stress-free and easy, and everyone loves them. They are definitely crowd "wowers!"

I think every woman has her likes and dislikes in the cooking world. Because my mom, mother-in-law and grandma were such great cooks, I grew to love cooking. Plus, I loved to eat so I learned to cook at an early age out of preservation!

Then, as a bored housewife, I took years of cooking classes. So, I can now do it all, from butchering half a cow to making the best ice cream in the world. But I admit it: Salads are my weak point. Here are some salads that I use to keep my weakness a secret from my guests.

*Grandma Freund, Mom, Dad, Dick and me*

# The Wedge

This one is so easy, I'm almost embarrassed! But it's such a pretty presentation, and I've found that my guests really, really love it!

1 head of iceberg lettuce
1 pound of bacon, fried crispy and broken up
2 tomatoes, cut into small chunks
Your favorite bleu cheese dressing

Cut a chilled head of lettuce into 4 or 6 wedges, depending on the size of the head. Put each wedge on its own individual plate. Drizzle bleu cheese dressing over the wedge. Decorate the wedge with tomato chunks and bacon pieces and serve!

Sometimes I like to let my guests decorate their own wedges. I'll cut up the wedges and put them on plates and put them back in the refrigerator to keep chilled. On the table I'll set a pretty ironstone pitcher full of bleu cheese dressing. In bowls with pretty serving spoons, I put the tomatoes and the bacon. When it's time for the salads, I deliver the plates to my guests and let them dress their own wedge. They love this!

# Seven-Layer Salad

My family loves this so much. It's a stress-buster because it has to be made the day before it is served.

1 cup sour cream

1 cup mayonnaise

Sugar to taste

1 head of iceberg lettuce, chopped into
   bite-sized pieces

2 tomatoes, chunked small

1 onion, chopped small

1 pound of bacon, fried and crumbled

1 bag of shredded cheddar cheese

1 small bag of frozen peas

2 green peppers, chopped small

In a large bowl, mix together the sour cream, mayo and sugar to taste. You don't want it to be too sweet, so you have to taste as you are adding. Set aside for a bit.

In a pretty, see-through glass serving dish, layer each of the other ingredients, starting with the lettuce and ending with the layer of green peppers. Then pour the dressing over the top, making sure to cover the entire green pepper layer. Cover and refrigerate for 24 hours before serving. During this time the dressing makes its way into all of the other layers. Oh wow . . . this is really good!

# Karin's World's Best Vinaigrette Dressing

I do have another trick to get out of salad duty: I invite people who make great salads over and have them bring the salads! My daughter-in-law, Karin, is a great salad maker. Her homemade balsamic vinaigrette dressing is the very best I have ever had. I had to pry the recipe from her, but because it was for my Quackers, she agreed to let me have it!

In a cruet, combine:

½ cup balsamic vinegar

¼ cup water

¼ cup or more extra virgin olive oil

Add 2 teaspoons Dijon mustard and shake to emulsify. Add to that 1 tablespoon honey and ¼ cup chopped parsley (fresh is best if you can get it!). You could also use any other herb that you like. If you can't get fresh, dried herbs are great too.

Add to this 1 shake of all-purpose seasoning and a dash of fresh ground pepper. Shake really well and refrigerate for at least an hour. Before serving, remove from refrigerator and allow to reach room temperature. This dressing is delicious on any kind of salad or vegetables, especially Caprese with tomato, mozzarella and fresh basil. It's also good on fruit salad.

# Family Fruit Salad

## Makes 8 servings

This is so sweet and delicious!

1 can (16 oz.) peach slices drained
2 sliced bananas
1 can (6 oz.) frozen lemonade, thawed
½ pint whipping cream
1 teaspoon sugar

Mash peaches and bananas until they are mushy. Stir in undiluted lemonade.

In a separate bowl, whip cream with sugar until thick and fold into the mashed fruit. Pour into a foil-lined loaf pan and cover. Freeze until firm.

Remove from the freezer a few minutes before you are ready to serve. Lay some lettuce on plates, and cut a slice of the fruit salad and place on top of lettuce. It's so pretty! Also, this will keep in your freezer for up to a month, so it's always handy.

# Chilled Pineapple Cake

This was one of my mom's favorite recipes.

For the filling:

Beat 3 egg yolks until thick. Add 6 tablespoons of sugar gradually until mixture is thick and lemon colored. Drain 1 can of crushed pineapple. Add 3 tablespoons of the syrup to the egg mixture. Cook the above in a double boiler until thickened. Stir as you would any custard. Stir continually and then cool.

Cream ¾ cup butter and add 1 cup powdered sugar gradually. Beat until light. Add the cooled custard and beat well. Beat 3 egg whites and a pinch of salt until stiff. Fold this into the custard mixture. Add drained pineapple and 1 tablespoon lemon juice. Fold in. Spread this on angel food cake cut into three layers. Frost with whipped cream. Allow to stand in refrigerator for an hour or more before serving.

quacky

Tip

I like to let this stay in the refrigerator longer than an hour if I have the time. The longer it sits, the better it gets!

# Chocolate Cream Puffs

**E**veryone has to have a killer cream puff recipe in their repertoire. It's not one I use often, but when I do it's the best. If you are not a chocolate fan, you can use caramel or butterscotch.

### Cream Puff Pastry:

¼ cup butter

½ cup water

½ cup flour

2 eggs, room temperature

Whipped cream

Preheat oven to 375 degrees. Boil water and butter in small saucepan. Remove from heat and add flour all at once, beating rapidly till dough leaves side of pan and forms a ball. If it doesn't ball up, put back on medium heat and keep beating. Cool for 5 minutes. Add eggs one at a time, beating frantically after each until dough is smooth. Drop small teaspoonfuls onto an ungreased cookie sheet 2 inches apart and bake for about 16 minutes in preheated oven till brown and puffed. Cool. Just before serving, fill with whipped cream by slicing off the very top and pulling out any wet filaments of dough. Spoon hot chocolate sauce over filled puffs, letting it dribble down the sides. Refrigerate if not serving right away.

Now, if you really want to be the "hostess with the mostest," fill the cream puffs with ice cream.

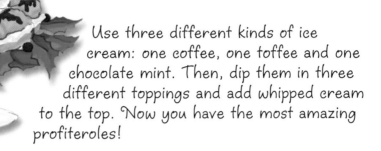

Use three different kinds of ice cream: one coffee, one toffee and one chocolate mint. Then, dip them in three different toppings and add whipped cream to the top. Now you have the most amazing profiteroles!

Chocolate Sauce:

3 ounces semisweet chocolate
2 tablespoons butter

Over low heat, melt chocolate and butter, stirring constantly. Sauce will thicken as it cools, so spoon over puffs quickly.

# Cream Cheese Snowmen

## Makes 3 dozen cookies

These really are the cutest cookies ever, and you can tell when they are done that they were all made with love.

1 package (8 oz.) cream cheese
1 cup powdered sugar
¾ cup butter or margarine
½ teaspoon vanilla
2 ¼ cups flour
½ teaspoon baking soda
Sifted powdered sugar
Miniature peanut butter cups
Assorted colored icing

Preheat oven to 325 degrees. Mix cream cheese, sugar, butter and vanilla with electric mixer on medium until well blended. Add flour and baking soda and mix well.

Shape dough into equal number of ½-inch and 1-inch balls. Using 1 small and 1 large ball per snowman, place balls slightly overlapping on an ungreased cookie sheet and squish to ¼-inch thickness.

Use a glass with flour on the bottom so it doesn't stick.
Keep doing this until you've used up all the balls.

Bake for 20 minutes or so or until light golden brown.
Remove from cookie sheet and place on a wire rack to cool.
Sprinkle with sifted powdered sugar and decorate with icing.
Cut peanut butter cups in half and use for hats. These are
too cute!

quacky
Tip

Wrap these in huge "poofs"
of cellophane and bring them
as hostess gifts. You'll be a
popular guest!

# Cream Cheesecake Dip

## Makes about 1½ cups

**S**ometimes I get cravings for cheesecake, but I don't have the patience to put one together. This dip is a great way to satisfy a cheesecake craving, and you can add any kind of fruit your cheesecake-needin' taste buds desire!

1 package (8 oz.) cream cheese, softened
1 jar (7 oz.) marshmallow creme

Mix cream cheese and marshmallow creme until well blended; refrigerate.

Serve with assorted fruit, pound cake, angel food cake or cookies. Yummy!

# Heath Bar Cake

## Makes 18 servings

I've always loved a Heath bar, but they can be really hard on your teeth! This is a wonderful way to get the flavor of toffee without fighting with a candy bar!

2 ¼ cups light brown sugar
½ cup margarine
2 cups plus 2 tablespoons flour
1 beaten egg
1 cup milk
1 teaspoon salt
1 teaspoon vanilla
1 teaspoon soda
6 Heath bars, crushed

Preheat oven to 350 degrees. Mix brown sugar, margarine and flour until crumbly. Reserve one cup for top. Beat egg and add milk, salt, vanilla and soda. Mix. Add brown sugar mixture and beat thoroughly. Pour batter into a greased and floured 9x13-inch pan. Put cup of crumbly mixture over the top and then sprinkle on the crushed Heath bars. Bake for 25 to 30 minutes.

You can cut these any way you like. Smaller pieces for finger food at a picnic, or larger pieces served with ice cream for dessert!

# Jeanne's Caramels

### Makes 3 dozen

Spread bottom and sides of a 9x5x3-inch loaf pan with butter. In a 2-quart saucepan, combine:

1 cup granulated sugar
½ cup light corn syrup
4 tablespoons butter
1 cup brown sugar
1½ cups light cream

Cook and stir over medium heat until sugars dissolve. Continue cooking, stirring occasionally to a firm ball stage (248 degrees). Remove from heat. Stir in 1 teaspoon vanilla. Turn into pan. Cool and cut into small squares. Wrap each one with wax paper, then twist the ends. Delicious!

# Macaroon Chocolate Chip Bars

## Makes 24 bars

½ cup butter
1 cup plus 2 tablespoons all-purpose flour, divided
1½ cups brown sugar, packed and divided
2 eggs
¼ teaspoon salt
1 cup chopped pecans
1½ cups flaked coconut
1 teaspoon vanilla extract
1 cup chocolate chips

Preheat oven to 325 degrees. Mix together butter, one cup flour and ½ cup brown sugar. Pat into the bottom of a 13 x 9-inch greased baking pan. Bake for 15 minutes. In a medium bowl, blend remaining flour and brown sugar, eggs, salt, pecans, coconut, vanilla and chocolate chips. Spread mixture onto baked crust. Bake for an additional 25 minutes. Cut into bars when cool.

# MaryAnn's Black Bottom Pie

Oh, how wonderful this is! I could probably go forever without chocolate, but this is one pie you will crave!

1 cup evaporated milk
1 envelope unflavored gelatin
$3/4$ cup sugar
$1/8$ teaspoon salt
$3/4$ cup milk
1 egg yolk
3 squares (1 oz. each) unsweetened chocolate
1 teaspoon vanilla
1 cup cream, whipped
1 baked 9-inch pie shell

Pour evaporated milk into freezer tray and let set half-hour in freezer. In the top of double boiler, mix gelatin, sugar and salt. Beat milk and egg yolk lightly and add to gelatin mixture. Add chocolate squares and cook over boiling water until chocolate is melted, stirring occasionally. Remove from heat and beat a few minutes until smooth. Chill until thickened. Whip evaporated milk and then fold into cooled mixture. Add vanilla. Pour into baked pie shell and refrigerate until ready to serve. Spread top with whipped cream. Shred chocolate over the top.

# Peanut Butter Hershey Kiss Cookies

2 ⅔ cups flour
2 teaspoons baking soda
1 teaspoon salt
1 cup butter
⅔ cup creamy peanut butter
1 cup sugar
1 cup brown sugar, firmly packed
2 eggs
2 teaspoons vanilla extract
Additional sugar
5 dozen Hershey Kisses, unwrapped

Preheat oven to 375 degrees. In a large bowl, mix flour, salt and baking soda. Add butter and peanut butter and mix until smooth. Add sugars and beat until light and fluffy. Add eggs and vanilla and mix until smooth.

Make small balls using level tablespoons of dough—add flour if needed. Roll in sugar.

Bake 2 inches apart on ungreased cookie sheet for 8 minutes.

Remove from oven and add one Kiss to the center of each cookie. Return to the oven and bake for 2 more minutes.

# Seven-Layer Cookie

## Makes 2 dozen

Easy and soooo delicious. What more can I say about these?

½ cup butter, melted
1 cup graham crackers, crushed
1 cup coconut
1 cup butterscotch chips, optional
1 cup chocolate chips
1 cup chopped nuts
One 15-oz. can sweetened condensed milk

Preheat oven to 350 degrees. Combine melted butter with graham cracker crumbs in 9x13-inch pan. Press firmly into pan. Layer in order: the coconut, butterscotch chips, chocolate chips and nuts. Pour sweetened condensed milk evenly over all ingredients. Bake for 25 to 30 minutes.

# Snickerdoodle Cookies

## Makes about 6 dozen cookies

These are a family favorite and a cookie exchange favorite. Personally, I just like saying the word "snickerdoodle"!

1 cup butter or margarine, softened
1 ½ cups sugar
2 eggs
1 teaspoon baking soda
2 ¾ cups all-purpose flour
¼ teaspoon salt
2 teaspoons cream of tartar
½ cup sugar with 2 teaspoons cinnamon mixed in

Preheat oven to 400 degrees. Cream together the butter and sugar. Add the eggs one at a time, mixing well after each one. Mix all dry ingredients together and add them to the egg mixture ⅓ at a time, mixing well after each addition. Cookie dough will be soft and sticky. Refrigerate the dough for at least 1 hour. Shape the dough into small balls (the size of a large marble) and roll them in cinnamon sugar. Place them on a parchment paper-lined cookie sheet about 2 inches apart and flatten them slightly. Cookies will spread out as they bake. Bake for 10 to 12 minutes or until lightly browned around the edges, but still soft. Remove from cookie sheet immediately (they will stick if allowed to cool on cookie sheet).

# Snowmen Cookies

## Makes 32 cookies

These cute snowmen cookies make great treats for children's parties. Kids are always willing to chip in and help decorate them!

1 package 16-oz. Nutter Butter cookies
1 ¼ pounds white candy coating, melted
Miniature chocolate chips
M&Ms miniature baking bits
Pretzel sticks, halved
Orange and red decorating gel or frosting

Using tongs, dip cookies in candy coating; shake off excess. Place on waxed paper. Place two chocolate chips on one end of cookies for eyes. Place baking bits down the middle of the cookie for buttons. For arms, dip the ends of two pretzel stick halves into coating; attach one to each side. Let stand until hardened. Pipe the nose and scarf with gel or frosting.

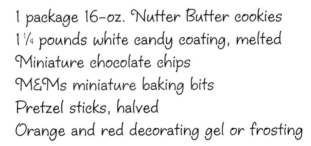

# Conclusion

## Make Every Day Christmas Day

Christmas is a very special day. You say the word and everyone smiles. Hopefully we all have some great memories of this feel-good day, a time when loved ones come from near and far. Maybe it's the only time of the year when the whole family is able to be together. It's a celebration. Life is to be celebrated. Don't lose that!

I say we should have the childlike joy of Christmas in every day. We only get to go through this life once. We have a choice: every day can be like Christmas, or every day can be a day of a long list of chores. Which sounds better to you?

I'm picking Christmas! Celebrate each day . . . good or bad. You'll have a great life, and it will all be wrapped up in Christmas bows. Believe in the magic!

> *"Christmas waves a magic wand*
> *over the world, and behold, everything*
> *is softer and more beautiful."*
>
> —Norman Vincent Peale

# Quacker Factory

# Christmas

## Recipe List

### Appetizers

# Beverages

# Breakfast

# Cookies

# Desserts

# Entrees

# Salads and Dressings

# Sides

# Soups

# Breads

# Acknowledgments

Tim and Lee, for the great memories you've created with me . . . we've survived and made new ones.

My friends, you've decorated with me, partied with me and loved me through it all. Thanks, I love you, too.

Susan, for decorating with me every day of the year.

HCI, for accepting me back with charm, grace and a great deal of love and talent.

Allison, Larissa and Lawna, thanks to all of you, I've never been so bedecked and bedazzled.

Kate and Lori, you guys make each day seem like a holiday.

QVC, you see my vision. David and Chris, you bought my vision.

Jodi, thank you for "getting" me.

My daughter-in-law, Karin, and her family, who share my Christmases now and make them memorable.

My brother, for sharing so many Christmases with me—good and bad—let's keep doing it.

# The Factory that Jeanne Built

In the mid-seventies, Jeanne Bice was like many women: a homemaker, a wife and mother. She was also a gourmet cook, a crafter, a party-thrower, a shopper, and on top of it...Bored with a capital "B." While bad news for her, it was great news for a future gaggle of "Quackers."

This boredom led Jeanne to partner with her friend to open a gift shop. After a year or two, what started out as a hobby became serious business when tragedy struck: Jeanne's business partner divorced and Jeanne's husband passed away unexpectedly, leaving her the sole source of support for her two children.

The women put their heads together to increase profits. They began producing a line of appliquéd clothing, and Jeanne Bice officially became a clothing designer. Soon after, Jeanne's partner remarried and left the business.

One day, trying frenetically to meet a deadline, Jeanne burst out: "I feel like I'm going Quackers!" The saying stuck and what millions of people know today as the Quacker Factory was born.

Jeanne and her family began to explore the "new frontier" of television shopping. Jeanne first appeared on QVC on February 4th, 1995, debuting her clothes and her now-famous "Quack" greeting. Not only did her entire line of clothes sell out in an unprecedented few minutes of air time, women all over the country literally started "Quacking" back to her—on the air, at the supermarket, at bookstore appearances.

Today, Jeanne is one of the most popular guests on QVC and the Quacker Factory is a multi-million-dollar business. In turn, the incredible gifts her loyal fans have brought to her are beyond her imagination, and she is continually awed by the special group of women who call themselves "Quackers."